Angel of Orphans

The story of R' Yona Tiefenbrunner
and the hundreds he saved

Angel of Orphans

The story of R' Yona Tiefenbrunner
and the hundreds he saved

MALKY WEINSTOCK

A TARGUM PRESS BOOK

First published 2009

ISBN 978-1-56871- 512-4

Published and distributed by:
TARGUM PRESS, INC.
22700 W. Eleven Mile Rd.
Southfield, MI 48034
E-mail: targum@targum.com
Fax: 888-298-9992
www.targum.com

Distributed by:
FELDHEIM PUBLISHERS
208 Airport Executive Park
Nanuet, NY 10954

Printed in Israel by Chish

ISRAELITISCHE ORTHODOXE GEMEENTE
MACHSIKE HADASS

JACOB JACOBSSTRAAT 22 2018 ANTWERPEN
TEL. 03/233.55.67 FAX 03/233.87.97

Antwerp, 14 May 2009

REF:

It was a great moment when we learned that the memory of a noble *askan* of our community — the unassuming Reb Yona Tiefenbrunner, *zt"l* — is to be shared with the public. On behalf of the entire Kehilla Machsike Hadass of Antwerp, we want to pay tribute here to this special person, a Jew who lived in our midst and then suddenly passed away at a young age nearly fifty years ago.

Very few members of our community still remember the astonishing *mesiras nefesh* of this man during World War II. With single-minded determination, Reb Yona dedicated himself heart and soul to many orphans during the war at great personal peril and raised them *al taharas hakodesh*. Later, Reb Yona was extremely influential in rebuilding the post-war Antwerp Jewish community.

For our Machsike Hadass community, for the Jewish communities around the world today boasting the families of the children Reb Yona always called his own, and in whose path and light they followed, let us give thanks and praise to Reb Yona. May he be a *meilitz yosher* for all those who were privileged to come in contact with this outstanding person.

In the name of the Kehilla,

S. Lehrer
Shlomo Zalmen Lehrer
Rosh Hakohol

Pinches Kornfeld
Chairman

לזכר נשמות

יונה בן אפרים ז"ל
פסח בן אפרים ז"ל

I wish to dedicate this book to the memories of my great-uncle Yona and his brother, Phillip Tiefenbrunner, my grandfather, to whom I owe the set of values that resulted in a deep appreciation of their supreme dedication to Torah and mitzvos amidst daily *mesiras nefesh*. For the benefit of our generation, which finds it close to impossible to relate to the *mesiras nefesh* of the previous generation, I was further motivated to intensely research and publicize this story in full detail.

While my great-uncle and grandfather were sparkling gems with many wonderful attributes, particularly their warmth and congeniality toward all, I've singled out their attribute of *mesiras nefesh* because of the relevance to this book.

I'm sure that the publication of their unique life story will provide them with *nachas ruach* in *Olam Haba,* and I'm confident that their courage and *mesiras nefesh* and the eternal bond that they forged with their children will serve as a true inspiration and motivator to all those who read this story.

Zevi Freund

Appreciation

First and foremost, to Chani, my revered role model, partner, *eishes chayil,* and best friend, who humbly stands by my side as my wife and the mother of our children. May Hashem fulfill all her *tefillos* and noble aspirations.

To my beloved parents, Mr. Moshe and Mrs. Maggy Kompel, who were and remain my first and constant source of inspiration. They are geniuses in *chesed* and giants of action. May Hashem grant them years of *Yiddish nachas* and joy from children, grandchildren, and great-grandchildren.

To my in-laws, Mr. Avrumie and Mrs. Bella Schon, two special people whose devotion to *kibbud av va'eim* and to *chesed* is legendary.

And to the author of this book, Malky Weinstock, for dedicating herself wholeheartedly to this endeavor, bringing this book to life with profound love and devotion.

Last, but certainly not least, to my dear children, who provide me the greatest joy in life — Henny, Motti, Shana, Esti, Chaim Yehuda, Sarah, and Yoni. Their innocence and purity of character teaches me to be the best I can be and to always pursue what is right. May they be a source of *nachas* to the whole family.

המלאך הגואל אותי מכל רע יברך את הנערים ויקרא בהם שמי ושם אבותי...

Zevi Freund
Sivan 5769

We didn't appreciate the greatness of his personality, his openheartedness, his organizational and leadership skills, and the warmth he exhibited to the brokenhearted orphans who gathered under his wings. No, we weren't cognizant of all of this as little kids, but we loved him like a father, uncle, and grandfather all in one. He gave us the will to continue with our lives. He restored the human spirit within each of us after the desolation of the Holocaust. We are all a living monument to his blessed memory.

— Moniek Kerber, one of Yona Tiefenbrunner's children from the Tiefenbrunner Home

CONTENTS

Preface 15
Acknowledgments 17
Prologue 21

1: Childhood Days 25

2: Colliding with Destiny. 35

3: Winds of War 41

4: New Arrivals 53

5: One Large Family 61

6: Facing the Monster: Gestapo Visits 69

7: Liberation: Not a Moment Too Soon 79

8: Who Is That British Soldier? 85

9: A New Chapter 93

10: Is It Possible to Sing? 101

11: A Promise with No Expiration Date 119

12: Always His Children 131

13: How Could the Heart that Beat for Others Stop Beating? 147

Epilogue 151

Through a Child's Eyes: The True Account of Aron Peterfreund 157

Bibliography 173

Preface

The fantastic array of Jewish institutions that flourish throughout the world today is stunning in its breadth and scope. Which begs the question: How is it possible that Jews have risen to distinction from the ashes of the *churban* of Europe in only a little over fifty years? Given the almost total devastation of our people, the achievements are completely disproportionate! It should have taken hundreds of years to rebuild *am Yisrael* after such devastating destruction.

Through the focus of a high-powered lens, we can detect the strands of an explanation. The *rabbanim* and *gedolim* who miraculously survived the war and rebuilt *am Yisrael* arrived, like so many others, on foreign shores bereft of family, funds, and community. The one thing they possessed in abundance was *mesiras nefesh*, self-sacrifice. They set their sights on the loftiest goals, and incredibly, despite the naysayers who mocked their grandiose visions, went on to found world-renowned Torah and communal institutions.

How to account for their legendary successes — which bordered on the miraculous — other than that it was through a hefty does of *siyatta diShmaya*, heavenly assistance? As the devastation of the Holocaust utterly defied logic in its depravity, with no other explanation than that it had to have been divinely ordained and orchestrated, the rebuilding was wrought by the Hand of Hashem beyond the confines of man and time. Could we not then conclude that the human artisans whom Hashem selected to perform His work of rebuilding were those who manifested a staunch sense of *mesiras nefesh*?

This book chronicles the riveting story of one such *mesiras nefesh* Jew. Yona Tiefenbrunner was an unsung hero who unwaveringly answered to a higher calling: for over two decades, from 1939 to 1962, he was the "father" of Holocaust orphans in Belgium in the face of formidable odds.

To get a sense of his accomplishments, turn the clock back to 1945. Throughout the war (and for many years after) Yona sheltered under his wing many shattered children, from toddlers to teens, bereft of family and stripped of *Yiddishkeit*. Were anyone to tell you then that many of these orphans would not only mature intact in spirit and *Yiddishkeit*, but also raise families who today, only sixty years later, are the pride of the Torah world, the idea would have been inconceivable.

Yona's *mesiras nefesh* enabled him to fashion of these broken shards a solid foundation that yielded prolific returns. Do not each one of us have a unique role to fulfill in building a stronger *am Yisrael*? We can all take heart from Yona's incredible story. It is a how-to guide for our own success stories, so that we, too, can be defined by what we pass on to the next generation.

Acknowledgments

First and foremost, my soul sings a song of praise to my Creator, who has graced me with singular compassion and Divine Providence in bringing this two-year-long endeavor to fruition. When I saw no end to the labyrinth of research required of me as an emissary to bring this story to light, He armed me with the stamina and fortitude to keep moving forward; another page, another vignette. When the time for publishing arrived, He orchestrated events to match the manuscript with the publisher.

No memoir of this scope is the work of one person. I want to extend my sincerest gratitude to Mr. Zevi Freund, a dear family friend, for presenting me with the opportunity to write this book, guiding me on the path that has led me to this high point in my writing career. A visionary like his great-uncle Yona, Zevi not only recognized my potential, but also the value and importance of documenting history.

I am indebted to my editor, Suri Brand, for providing some of the best analysis and editing around, and to the rest of the team at Targum Press, especially Allison Fried and Beena Sklare, for their stellar work in all the other aspects of publication.

I am grateful to the Tiefenbrunner family — Joseph and Judith Schreiber, Jeannette Rushy, and Marriette Lipschutz — for granting me the privilege of perpetuating their father's legacy, and for the many hours they spent with me personally, sharing their memories and their photos.

I am indebted to Mr. Monju Tiefenbrunner, Yona's elder brother and the sole surviving member of the family, who graciously shared the details of his early family life and ancestry, both in a personal interview and by sharing with me his self-published autobiography, *A Long Journey Home*. May the Almighty grant him life, health, and *nachas* from his family.

This book grew out of the over fifty interviews I had the good fortune of conducting with former children and staff members of the Tiefenbrunner Home. To all who invited me to their homes, who spent long hours with me on long-distance and overseas phone calls, who contributed their photos, documents, and letters and otherwise pointed me in the direction of further research, I would like to extend a very special thank you. You will see your influences throughout this book. I am truly humbled by your life stories and the perseverance and determination you had to move on with your lives.

Although all the names are too numerous to mention, this book could not have happened without the passionate enthusiasm, abundance of research information, guidance, and perspective (which is reflected in the preface) of a true friend and mentor, the esteemed Rebbetzin Bracha Biegeleisen, a child survivor of Bergen-Belsen and later a child of the Tiefenbrunner Home.

A special thank you goes out to Aron Peterfreund, a Belgian native who spent years in the Tiefenbrunner Home and who presently lives in Belgium. In addition to serving as a terrific motivator for this project, Aaron provided a world of insight into Jewish Belgium, past and present. His personal narrative appears at the end of this book.

To my beloved parents, Rabbi and Mrs. Yaakov and Shulamis Bluming, who are each lifelong models of *mesiras nefesh* for Torah. As of the publication of this book, the pain of the recent loss of my father-in-law, Reb Baruch Weinstock, *zt"l*, is still great. His response to illness didn't create his greatness; it just revealed what had been there throughout his life. I grieve that he couldn't be around to witness this achievement, of which we often spoke. His passion for unflinchingly living life according to Torah principles without fame or fanfare has inspired my own passion in completing this documentary of a man who embodied similar goals.

My wonderful mother-in-law, Sarah Weinstock, has personally demonstrated to me the meaning of endurance, with her outstanding grace and dignity throughout this difficult period. May Hashem grant her many delightful years of *nachas* from her children and grandchildren.

Last and most of all, I want to thank my dear husband, Menachem, whose encyclopedic knowledge of world history has had a profound effect on the book's content and organization. My children, Esty, Miriam, and Gedalia, all contributed to the joy and anticipation of this project, and I thank them for their love and support. May our family always merit to personify the ideals of Yona Tiefenbrunner.

Prologue

Brussels, 1942

The little boy's face was twisted in fear. He had heard from others that no one left this place alive. There was no one left to save him, for his parents had already been taken away.

Suddenly, he heard footsteps descending the stairs. *They're coming to get me now!* his tortured mind screamed.

There was nowhere to hide. He retreated to the furthest corner, curling up like a frightened kitten. His eyes were shut tightly, his head buried in his folded arms, willing away his tormentors, yet bracing for the inevitable onslaught.

"*Gut Shabbos*," said a gentle voice.

A "*gut Shabbos*" greeting in the cellar of the Gestapo? Why was his mind tormenting him now? He remained motionless, frozen.

"*Gut Shabbos*! I'm here to take you to safety. Take my hand!"

The words gently floated into unbelieving ears.

He had forgotten it was Shabbos! He had only known that today was the End.

He lifted his face an inch from his folded arms, afraid to look, afraid that his eyes might deceive him.

But there before him, incredibly, stood a kind-looking Jew dressed in Shabbos attire with his hand outstretched.

"You are free now! We're going to my house. It is a safe place. There are other children just like you there. They are all waiting for you!"

Something deep inside the boy made him trust the kindly Jew.

And just like that, he walked with the man out of that terrible place and back into life...

Israel, 2007

I sit in a living room in Ra'anana, Israel, with three sisters. They are showing me several of their family albums bulging with aging black-and-white photos of their father with groups of smiling children.

They hand me a pamphlet with the heading "*Liste Des Anciens Du Home*" (List of the old children of the home). Scanning the pages, I notice it is an alphabetized listing with over one hundred names, complete with addresses and phone numbers. They are common Jewish surnames... Amsel, Berkowitz, Birnbaum and Bornstein, Singer, Stern, Weinberg, Zucker.

But this is no ordinary class or grade list. These names — which I am told correspond with many of the faces in the albums — were those of the orphans and staff members of the World War II Belgian orphanage directed by Reb Yona Tiefenbrunner, *zt"l*.

I stare at the photos of this kind-looking Jew, who had been the father of two hundred orphans. Something deep inside me says that there is a legendary epic of *mesiras nefesh*, long forgotten, that needs to be told. The photos and phone numbers on those pages are my trail.

Many months later, in the course of my research, I chance upon a virtual tour of the National Monument to the Jewish martyrs of Belgium, an impressive-looking monument located in the Belgian Anderlicht district. Thousands of names stretching as far as my eyes can see — 23, 838 names I learn later — are inscribed on the monument walls. I can't help but notice once again surnames so common and familiar — Wulliger, Rosner,

Miller, Mandel, Singer, Rosengarten, Rosenfeld. So many Jewish names that resonate with me... I have friends, neighbors, with those very names!

And just as rapidly, another thought follows in its wake: the much smaller list of similar names now in my possession. But my list chronicles names that lived and flourished, thanks to Yona Tiefenbrunner. My list is a list of people whom I have personally visited or contacted by phone or e-mail; the others are names that will be forever silent. This book, then, is a monument to Yona Tiefenbrunner, who created a living legacy for Belgian Jewry and beyond.

1
Childhood Days

They named him Yona.

As with every new child, they celebrated his birth, welcoming this newborn son as the harbinger of *mazel* and good fortune into their home — and at his bris, they called him Yona.

If when naming a child every parent is endowed — however unwittingly — with a divine sense that renders the given name completely apt to the soul and character of the child, Yona's name could not have been more prescient. Like the bird in flight, the little baby named Yona would one day play an invaluably heroic role in history, rescuing over two hundred Jewish souls under his wings of courage and heroism.

And like the biblical *yonah*, the dove that selflessly left the safety of Noach's ark, flying into the tempest to see whether the devastating flood waters had abated, Yona would repeatedly enter the Nazi storm, providing shelter that bordered on the miraculous.

Yona was born on a summer's day, June 18, 1914 (24 Sivan 5674), in Wiesbaden, Germany. Reb Efroim and Matel Tiefenbrunner were already blessed with a son and a daughter, but Yona was their first child born on German soil, where Reb Efroim had moved his young family only two years before in 1912.

Reb Efroim came from a family of Sanzer chassidim in the Polish shtetl of Limanowa. He had been a child prodigy, exhibiting a keen ability and desire for learning. So extraordinary was his acquisition of knowledge and memory that of all his brothers, he alone had been chosen by his parents to continue learning, while the others would learn a profession. In the *beis midrash* of Sanz where he studied, the young chassid quickly gained renown as a young *ilui*. Reb Efroim knew virtually the entire *Shas* by heart!

Yona's parents, Mrs. Matel Tiefenbrunner and Rav Efroim Tiefenbrunner, Hy"d

At the age of twenty-one, in 1908, Reb Efroim married eighteen-year-old Matel Licht of Tarnow. During those years preceding World War I, shtetl life in Poland was rife with financial hardship. Many Jewish families left their parents and extended families behind to migrate to Germany where living conditions were easier. In 1912, Reb Efroim joined the other immigrants and moved his young family to Wiesbaden, where a number of Matel's family members had already established themselves and the promise of better opportunities beckoned.

Wiesbaden was a resort town, the therapeutic value of its natural hot springs accounting for a very large population of over 200,000 residents and an even larger crowd of regular tourists. At the turn of the twentieth century, the summer months of July and August even brought wealthy American Jews to vacation there, and two kosher hotels had sprung up to host them. The Wiesbaden that the Tiefenbrunners came to also began seeing an influx of Jewish immigrants from Eastern Europe, swelling the small Jewish community that had existed since the fourteenth century. Most were merchants, who recognized opportunity in the ready marketplace of all the spa patrons and employees, and operated small shops and kiosks to serve them.

Reb Efroim's vast Talmudic knowledge could have earned him a position in the Wiesbaden rabbinate. His modesty and humility deterred him. Instead, he sat and learned while his wife ran their business of selling textiles — bolts of fabric, tablecloths, linens — to the neighboring farming community.

The family grew. In addition to his older siblings, Avraham Yaakov and his sister Sala, Yona was joined by six more in close succession: Maurice, two years his junior; Phillip, whose twin brother died in infancy; Osias; Rosel; and Lina.*

Yona was a solidly built, muscular child. His physical strength was matched by a brave and spunky spirit, a combination that compelled him to protect his weaker siblings from the bullying of others, particularly his non-Jewish peers in school. In Germany, school attendance was mandatory, and since there was no Jewish school in Wiesbaden, Yona and his siblings attended the non-Jewish public school. Very few of the eight hundred students that made up the student body were Jewish, and Yona and his brothers were at a decided disadvantage. What's more, already in the 1920s, anti-Semitism was rearing its ugly head, manifesting itself in frequent anti-Semitic incidents in school. Forced to stoically bear ridicule from teachers and fend off the jeers and beatings from students, Yona was hardened at a young age to a bleak reality.

Relief came in the early evenings when Yona and his siblings attended cheder, and on Shabbos, when, of course, they would not attend school. A sympathetic non-Jewish friend agreed to bring them the missed class work on Sunday morning so they could catch up with their studies in time for Monday's lessons.

Although they had very few school friends, the Tiefenbrunner children had several Jewish friends in the neighborhood — the Reisels, the Lerners, the Kannels. Originally from Russia, the Kannel family was quite well-to-do. The Tiefenbrunners loved to go visit them and play with their large collection of toys. To the children's regret, the Kannels left for Palestine in the early 1930s.

---

* Of the entire family, only Yona and two of his brothers, Maurice and Phillip, would survive the Holocaust.

Yona was but a youngster, when, shortly after World War I, his father suddenly became blind, the result of an illness that would easily be correctable today. Reb Efroim was not quite forty when he lost his sight. To compound matters, much of the country was in financial turmoil after losing the war, and large swathes of the country were occupied by French and British troops. Many people, as is always the case under such conditions, speculated and made fortunes, but the Tiefenbrunners were not among them.

They were too proud to accept handouts, so Reb Efroim opened a kosher grocery/delicatessen selling kosher items like butter, cheese, and deli meats. He was aided by his noble wife, who bore the primary burden of running the business. Reb Efroim's piety and scrupulousness earned them many customers, especially during the Pesach season, when kashrus was such a crucial issue.

With Mother busy in the shop, Yona's oldest sister, Sala, assumed responsibility for running the household. The younger children revered her, knowing that she had to give up much of her free time to cook and do the mending or the laundry. Often, she didn't attend school or visit with friends because there was work to do at home.

And so, from early on, Yona and his siblings absorbed the lessons of loyalty, hard work, and selfless dedication. In those days, most customers did not carry their purchases home. It was expected that the grocer would take their orders and deliver the goods later on credit, and, not unlike today, have to pursue the customers to pay up their balances. The children would help make deliveries to customers and collect money.

The community was spread out all over the town, so it was not easy to fulfill these tasks. Early every morning, Yona and his brothers would go off to school, and upon returning at lunchtime, they headed straight for their duties in the shop. The little ones towed the small grocery cart laden with heavy groceries. Later on, bicycles replaced the cart as a means of transport. In the early evening, their duties completed, they would head to the cheder for lessons. They would return home at last after a very long day, too exhausted to do homework, which then had to be crammed in early the next morning before school and the looming prospect of another hectic afternoon.

Certainly, though, the stresses armed Yona for what was to come later. His noble parents, who never succumbed to despair despite their hardships, endowed him with a formidable legacy of invincible faith and courage.

Growing up in his parents' home also fortified Yona with the importance of Torah learning. Although a shopkeeper, Reb Efroim utilized his gift of prolific memory and knowledge and strongly committed himself to the needs of his community members. He would avail himself readily to give guidance to all who sought it. So well did his photographic memory of *Shas* and *poskim* serve him that, despite his blindness, he could give *shiurim* to the young and old. The most memorable were his annual *derashos* on Shabbos Shuvah and Shabbos HaGadol.

In time, Reb Efroim gained recognition not only as an expert in halachic matters, but also as a mentor in day-to-day issues. He was often approached by *rabbanim* from neighboring communities who sought his counsel.

During the summers of 1929, '30, and '31, the venerated Bobover Rebbe, Rabbi Benzion Halberstam, *Hy"d*, came to vacation at the mineral baths of Wiesbaden, and it was in the Tiefenbrunner home that he

Yona, age 14 (first on the left), with friends, August 1930

and his entourage stayed. Reb Efroim had studied with the Rebbe in the Sanzer *beis midrash* years before, and this was the only private home in Wiesbaden where the Rebbe felt comfortable relying on the kashrus.

In 1931, Yona left for yeshivah in nearby Frankfurt (a distance of fewer than fifteen miles) to pursue his Torah studies under the leadership of Rav Yosef Breuer,* grandson of Rabbi Shamshon Rafael Hirsch, *zt"l*. Yona dormed there, occasionally returning for Shabbos.

Oh, those sweet days spent poring over the Gemara in the company of friends! Alas, they wouldn't last.

Yona disembarked from the train one Friday morning on a visit home from yeshivah for Shabbos. His ears were assailed by a thunderous booming voice issuing a stream of words that he couldn't make out. His questing eyes quickly latched onto the town hall, the source of the tumult. From the distance, he could make out brown uniformed young men shouting unfamiliar slogans. Dozens of brown uniforms from which hands and feet emanated were strutting about. Drawing closer, his gaze reached their faces. Faces he knew! They were faces that belonged to his classmates, neighbors, and friends who had joined the Hitler Youth group, the Nazi party's official youth organization.

During the immediate post–World War I years, the Jews of Wiesbaden had maintained cordial relations with their gentile neighbors. But with the Nazi party's rise to power in the early 1930s came rallies, marches, blood-red banners, flags emblazoned with the swastika, and speeches broadcast on loudspeakers in the marketplace — a well-orchestrated marketing blitz to spread their pernicious propaganda and poison the local population's minds against the Jews.

"Let's go, Maurice," nudged Yona when he reached home at last. "Let's go find out what all the noise is about!"

The two brothers stole into the hall, which was by then bustling with over one hundred Germans. Raucous laughter and shouts of "Attack the Jews! Destroy their businesses!" filled the cavernous room.

"Look what we have here — two of our very own nosy Jew boys!"

It took only a split second for Yona to register that Kurt, a friend with whom he'd often gone bike riding and walked home from school, was now sporting the Hitler Youth uniform and cruelly betraying him

* Rav Breuer survived the war and ultimately came to America, settling in the Washington Heights neighborhood of New York City, where he founded K'hal Adas Yeshurun, also known as the Breuer's Kehilla.

and Maurice. But a split second was too late; the two brothers were set upon by the frenzied mob, and, badly bruised and beaten, they were thrown out.

While they boasted that they'd "attended" a Nazi meeting, Yona and his brother learned firsthand that his close friends were now foes. Wiesbaden, as all of Germany, was no longer a safe home for Jews.

When Yona returned to Frankfurt after Shabbos, he joined the Poalei Agudah youth movement in Frankfurt,* attending their regularly scheduled Torah and agricultural training classes in preparation for aliyah to Palestine. It wasn't coincidental that Yona met Ruth Feldheim at those meetings, the young woman who would later become his wife and his partner in his life's work.

"Freedom and Bread! Freedom and Bread!"

Hitler's political campaign slogan resounded throughout Germany during the elections of 1933. His appeal to the lower and middle classes and his charismatic oratory and propaganda that resonated with believers in nationalism, anti-Semitism, and anti-Communism accounted for Hitler's meteoric rise to power.

Hitler wasted no time in issuing laws and decrees of ostracization and social discrimination against German Jews, in the attempt to make life so unpleasant for them that they would emigrate. The campaign started on April 1, 1933, when a one-day boycott of Jewish-owned shops took place. Suddenly, Jews were no longer welcome in schools and universities, even in shops and restaurants. Placards reading "Jews not admitted" and "Jews enter this place at their own risk" began to appear all over. In some parts of the country, Jews were even banned from public parks, swimming pools, and public transportation.

Germans were also encouraged not to purchase goods from Jewish companies or use Jewish doctors and lawyers. Jewish civil servants, teachers, and those employed by the mass media were summarily dis-

* Poalei Agudah was an organization for Orthodox Jewish youth prior to the war. It espoused settling the Land of Israel and conducted regular meetings and organized groups to train its young members in farming and raising crops.

missed. In 1935, the Nuremberg Laws on Citizenship and Race were passed: Jews could no longer be citizens of Germany. The degradation of the limitations and restrictions heaped upon them propelled many Jews to leave Germany for Palestine, England, France, or the United States.

Soon the Tiefenbrunners' delicatessen was struggling. More and more of their customers had either left or were experiencing their own financial hardships and were hard-pressed to pay their bills.

In the minds of people who remained, Yona's family among them, the Nazis were a temporary aberration. Soon, they believed, the Germans would realize that they had made a political error. Hitler was a madman, they agreed, a temporary menace. They would wait it out, trying as those times were, until better times returned.

Since the family business could no longer sustain them, the young Tiefenbrunner teenagers — Yona, Maurice, and Phillip — had no choice but to assume financial responsibility and seek employment in Jewish-owned businesses. With a heavy heart, Yona came home from yeshivah to work in a film factory. Maurice was a warehouse manager in a large department store. Phillip left in 1936 for Antwerp to stay with an aunt. Working there in the scrap-metal trade, he sent his wages home to help support his parents.

In 1937, Yona, an idealistic young man of twenty-three who was already very active in Poalei Agudah, sensed the stirrings of an inner calling. He wanted to teach Jewish children. Against the better judgment of his family, who felt that the difficult times mandated his continued employment, Yona left his factory job for the Jewish Teacher's College in Cologne to receive training. From there he went on to attend the rabbinical seminar of Berlin.

Who knew that obtaining his credentials as a teacher was another piece in his destiny as savior of so many Jewish children?

Yona was away in yeshivah on October 28, 1938, the day that his parents and siblings were officially expelled from Germany. They were arrested with hundreds of other Polish Jewish families and crammed into a train, which dumped them somewhere right past the Polish border.

This is how Hitler forcibly moved hundreds of thousands of Jews eastward into Poland. Always clinging to hope, they believed that they would find safety from the anti-Semitic virus that had infected all of the Nazi movement. Instead, they would find themselves trapped by the Nazis in Eastern Europe and later crammed into ghettoes, followed by ghetto liquidation and eventually mass murder in the death camps.

Yona at twenty years old, 1934

Shortly after, in early November 1938, aware of the imminent danger of deportation to an uncertain fate, Yona managed to smuggle across the German border into Belgium to join his brother Phillip in Antwerp. With the exception of Maurice, who also survived by fleeing Poland to Belgium, the rest of the family — Reb Efroim, Matel, and the remainder of his siblings, including Avraham Yaakov and Sala, who had already married and established homes of their own — ultimately perished in Auschwitz.

2

Colliding with Destiny

For the first time in his life, Yona found himself a refugee. But he didn't dwell on that for long; there was too much to do! His arrival in Belgium had coincided closely with a very specialized group of refugees: trainloads of German *Judishe Kinder*, Jewish children. They were part of the *Kindertransport* program, the rescue effort to save Jewish children from Nazi oppression, which began on December 1, 1938. Under this effort, Belgium had accepted over five hundred German and Austrian Jewish children.

Salvation for hundreds of refugee children from Germany begot a new pressing concern: housing them. A committee, the Belgian Welfare Committee for Jewish Children (WCJC), was hurriedly formed to address their needs. As a certified teacher with a degree, Yona was hired to found a youth home for teenage boys in Heide, a resort town just north of Antwerp, since there was already an existing yeshivah there that the boys could attend. Yona rented a house on Thillo Street and opened its doors to boys aged fifteen to seventeen.

The students, all of whom came from religious families, divided their time between work on nearby farms and study in the yeshivah. In the evenings, Dora Hausner, a colleague of Yona's from the Teachers' College of Cologne, taught the boys English. Dora had smuggled herself into Belgium in 1939 by hiding in a truck under sacks of potatoes.

Yona (in the center) with the children from the Heide home. The inscription on the back of the photo reads: "Unser Heim ('our home' in German), Heide, June 13, 1939."

Yona now had children to care for, but still no wife. It wasn't long before he was introduced to a young woman working as a cook in another children's home. Yona realized immediately that he knew her. It was Ruth Feldheim from Frankfurt, whom he had first met when they worked together in the Poalei Agudah meetings! As they renewed their acquaintance, he learned that she had been working in Dinslaken, Germany, in the orphanage of Dr. Rothschild. She, too, had fled to Antwerp in 1938 — along with Dr. Rothschild, his wife, and their two little daughters — and was working as a cook in the Antwerp orphanage the Rothschilds now directed.

Here in Antwerp, far from home, Yona knew that Hashem had sent him a wonderful gift. Both were of the same German-Yekkish background; both were committed to caring for Jewish children. It seemed like a match made in heaven. They were married in a simple wedding ceremony in Antwerp, on May 9, 1940 (2 Iyar 5700). They celebrated their wedding mostly with friends — neither had much family in Antwerp, with the exception of Yona's brother, Phillip, and his wife, Henny.

Yona with his boys in Heide

It was a sad honeymoon for the just-married Tiefenbrunners. Only one day after their wedding, on Friday, May 10, 1940, the Nazis — showing complete disregard for the neutrality of their western neighbors — invaded the Netherlands, Belgium, Luxembourg, and France. It would take the Nazis eighteen days to complete their occupation — eighteen days that the Belgian army still maintained hopes of fending them off. The young people returned to Heide that day and was immediately caught up in the ensuing political chaos. The moment they arrived at the Brussels railway station, Yona and Ruth were arrested by Belgian police. Ruth was a German citizen — the invading enemy! And Yona was taken for holding "stateless" (without any nationality) papers.

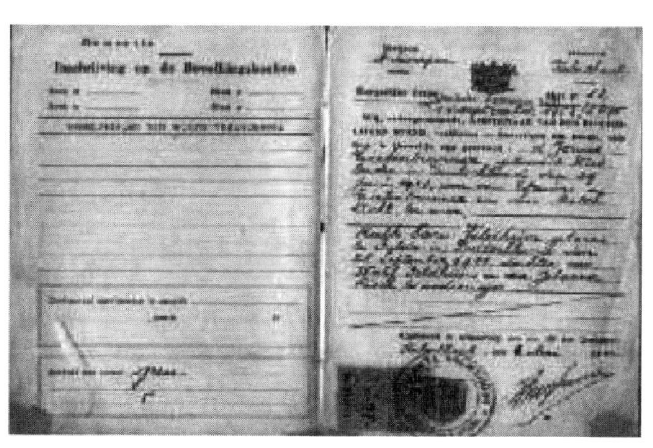

Yona and Ruth's marriage certificate, dated May 6, 1940. Ruth's name is written as "Ruth Sarah" — Hitler had decreed that all German Jews must append to their names either "Abraham" or "Sarah."

The police marched them through the streets of Brussels to the police station, where they joined other detainees. Toward evening, the men and women were separated and the women were freed. Fearfully, Ruth watched her new husband, Yona, being herded onto a truck with the other detainees. Rumors had it that they would be deported to Gurs, in neighboring France, an internment camp for Germans and pro-Nazis. This was where the Belgian army was deporting captured German soldiers.

Who knew what fate awaited him there?

Instinct had Ruth rushing to a nearby street vendor. She purchased three loaves of bread, which she quickly handed to Yona before he was led away from her and pushed onto the truck.

Where to go now? She would go to Rothschild's orphanage, Ruth decided. Returning to the train station, Ruth was once again arrested and brought to the same police station, but was summarily released. At last she made it to the Rothschild home in Antwerp at eleven o'clock that night. She found everyone sheltering in the cellar because of the heavy German bombardments.

The next morning, with the ominous droning of German planes overhead, Ruth contacted Phillip, Yona's brother, to fill him in on the events of the past twenty-four hours. Phillip and his wife were making plans to escape to Switzerland. Would Ruth join them? Tense moments ensued. To run or to stay and wait for her husband's uncertain return?

Loyalty won over fear, and Ruth — married only one day — declined the offer, preferring to wait for Yona in Belgium with Mrs. Rothschild. Her husband, a German citizen, had also been arrested by the Belgian government.*

Ruth's decision was rewarded very soon after. Days later, on May 13, all the detainees were released, and Yona was joyfully — if slightly subdued under the stress of those turbulent times — reunited with Ruth to begin their new life together.

The first order of business was to return to Heide, where Yona learned that the children had all dispersed. Immediately Yona set out on bicycle to find them. Some had joined the thousands of Jews fleeing to France, seeking shelter in small farms and villages; others never made it past the border. They had ended up in Ostende, a city on the Belgian coast. Yona found the children there and returned with them to Antwerp.

Reunited with his boys, Yona reestablished his orphanage in what had been an old-age home. A new routine was established. The boys studied in the neighboring yeshivah in the mornings, and in the afternoon they were apprenticed to local tradesman — tailors, bakers, and tanners — to learn and master a profession.

Yona's new children's home had no sponsors, as the WCJC could no longer provide funds, and the days that followed were financially trying. Yona and Ruth lacked even for the basic necessities to give the boys. Committed heart and soul to the welfare of the twenty boys under his care, and with no way to cover even the minimal expenses, Yona saw no other recourse but to seek help. He started fund-raising where he could, even walking as far as Brussels — a distance of some thirty miles — to

---

* Like Yona, Dr. Rothschild was deported by the Belgian army to Gurs with other German pro-Nazis, but succeeded in escaping to Switzerland. Upon returning to Antwerp in June 1945, he discovered his camera in the attic of his house with film that contained wedding photos of Yona and Ruth.

collect money. Sometimes he succeeded in obtaining a sum of money; other times, food-ration tickets.*

One day Yona returned home distraught — his fund-raising efforts has not been fruitful. His wife met him at the door with a smile and good news: help had come at last from an anonymous donor.

"A non-Jewish gentleman I did not recognize rang the bell earlier this afternoon," she told him. "He asked to come in and speak with me. He told me that he had heard about the dedication of my husband. Next thing I knew, he was handing me a large sum of money, but he refused to give me his name."

They never did discover the donor's identity. Sometimes they liked to speculate whether it was perhaps Eliyahu HaNavi in disguise. Regardless, they believed he was heaven-sent, and they thanked the One Above who sustains our every need, who saw to it that their financial worries were solved, for the moment.

* The occupation had led to a restriction of supplies that caused a shortage of food. Needing to ration the food supply, the Nazi occupational government issued food tickets that were to be exchanged for predetermined amounts of bread, vegetables, and other staples.

3
Winds of War

To flee or to stay? This ancient dilemma that has haunted persecuted Jews throughout the ages plagued Belgian Jewry now.

On the eve of the German invasion, the Belgian Jewish communities of Belgium's main cities, Brussels and Antwerp, numbered 85,000 Jews. Most did not hold Belgian citizenship; they were Eastern European Jews who had arrived in Belgium in the 1920s, fleeing pogroms and harsh living conditions. In the 1930s, came German Jews who fled Germany after Hitler's rise to power. By the late 1930s, Antwerp had developed a vibrant Jewish presence. It was home to five large shuls and twenty-eight *batei midrash* belonging to the various chassidic sects that had settled in the city — Czortkov, Belz, Gur, Vizhnitz, Sighet. The Agudath Israel movement was in full force; it had begun its activities as early as 1912. The community also boasted the twin educational institutions of Yesodei Hatorah for boys and the associated Bais Yaakov girls' school.* Both schools had stellar reputations that had spread beyond the borders of Belgium.

Now these once-strong communities were foundering. Mortal fear

---

* The boys' school was founded in 1903. The Bais Yaakov, founded in 1938, had replaced another girls' school that had been established in 1923.

had struck the Jews upon witnessing the German invasion. Thousands of Jews abandoned their homes, their shuls, and their businesses, fleeing the country overnight.

To where did they escape? They flocked to the border of France, taking advantage of the huge waves of refugees and the chaos that prevailed in the north of France before its defeat by the Germans. Once in France they headed for the south — not yet under official German occupation — where they hid in remote villages.

Nearly everyone Yona and Ruth knew was fleeing. But for them it was never a consideration. Possessed of the fiercest sense of duty, Yona and his wife opted to stay in order to look after the children. They knew that continuing to operate their children's home right under the noses of the advancing Germans meant the possibility of arrest and deportation at any moment. But attempting to flee with the children presented certain danger. The boys had little chance of escaping: because they were of German origin, between the German invasion and the French and Belgian capitulation they were certain to be apprehended at the French border.

The German occupational forces in Belgium did not begin their anti-Jewish persecutions immediately, and life, for the moment, seemed to resume its former routine. Most of the Jews who had fled to France returned. They feared internment by the German occupying forces in France, and the good news had come to them from Belgium: the Germans were not harassing the Jews who had remained behind. This contradicted reports from the East describing the sadistic actions and behavior of the Germans toward the Jews. But they chose not to believe the reports. They wanted to go home.

But in October 1940, the Germans changed their policy, and over a period of several months unleashed a flood of anti-Jewish measures.

The first prohibitions outlawed *shechitah* and other religious practices. The October decree additionally made it compulsory for Jews to register in a special "*Juden Register*" under the pretense of a census. The more wary Jews disobeyed the edict, but most of the population did not suspect the trap that would later facilitate their roundup and deportation to the death camps. Because the anti-Jewish orders were at first slow in coming, the Nazis achieved their goal of deluding the population at large into believing that Belgian Jews would not suffer.

Sure enough, other discriminatory actions followed, progressively turning the Jews into outcasts. Decrees were announced defining who was to be regarded as a Jew under the law. They had to have their identity cards stamped "*Juif-Jood*" (Jew.) They were barred from holding public office and from professions such as law, education, and the media.

On April 10, 1941, rioting broke out against the Jews in Antwerp.* Four days later, on April 14, another riot followed — a pogrom organized against the Jews of Antwerp by local pro-Nazi groups, with the assistance of the German forces. Two of Antwerp's most prominent shuls, the Van den Nestlei and Oostenstraat synagogues, were looted, and many Jewish-owned shops were burned down. The municipal council of Antwerp assumed responsibility for the attacks and attempted to refund the Jews for the damage, but the Germans blocked the implementation of the decision.

The "Aryanization of Jewish businesses" was the characteristically methodical and conniving way in which the Nazis gradually stole Jewish property and assets. In May 1941, Jews were ordered to clearly mark their businesses with signs in Flemish, French, and German, stating "Jewish-owned enterprise," so that the Germans could easily identify the businesses, which they would then appropriate. Jews were later ordered to declare their capital and other assets, including real estate, which were then confiscated. They were restricted to withdrawing only fixed minimal monthly amounts from their bank accounts — until their deportation, when the Nazis simply transferred the funds into their own accounts.

The harassment progressively worsened. As of August 29, 1941, Belgian Jews could no longer enter hotels, restaurants, and cafés. They could no longer stroll in public gardens or sit on public benches, and they were forbidden to own or make use of a radio. They were confined to only

* More than in other cities of Belgium, in Antwerp the Germans received the support and collaboration of local pro-Nazi and anti-Semitic parties and the Belgian authorities.

four Jewish communities in four major Belgian cities — Antwerp, Brussels, Liege, and Ghent — where they were subjected to a nightly curfew, from 8 p.m. to 7 a.m.

On November 25, 1941, the German occupation authorities ordered the Belgian Jews to establish the *Association des Juifs en Belgique* (Association of Jews of Belgium), or AJB. This was an official but captive Jewish organization created for the cynical purpose of having Jewish leaders serve as intermediaries in enforcing the anti-Jewish orders of the Nazi occupational authorities (similar to the ubiquitous *Judenrat*, which the Nazis mandated in every Jewish community they occupied). The AJB directed the execution of all German orders, regardless of the reservations they may have harbored. They believed the reigning fallacy of that time, that cooperating with, rather than opposing, the occupational government was the lesser of the two evils.

That same month, all Jewish children were expelled from the public schools.

The new year of 1942 ushered in only more hardship for Belgian Jewry. In January 1942, they were officially forbidden to leave the country, and by June all Jews were compelled to wear the Nazi-era symbol of the degradation of Jews, the yellow star. But none were prepared for the worst that was yet to come: deportation of all foreign-born Belgian Jews, which constituted the majority of Belgian Jewry at the time.

Deportation. To where? In July 1942, the Nazis had instituted the horrid deception of a Jewish "compulsory labor service."* "We need you to help us in your country of origin" was the trumped-up explanation to Belgium's Jews. And on July 25, 1942, the AJB delegates received the order that 12,000 Jews between the ages of fifteen and fifty must present themselves for "labor mobilization."

The AJB agreed to this, based on their already established policy of cooperation. They were trapped in their perception that the activities of the AJB could not but be carried out "within the framework of the Belgian laws and the directives of the occupation authorities." They were

* Michman, *Belgium and the Holocaust*, 355–60.

fearful of blind, wild roundups wreaking havoc in the community, and thus, in the interest of the general Jewish population, they saw no alternative other than absolute submission to German orders.

Their cooperation policy couldn't have proven more wrong, of course. The Nazi occupiers were exploiting the AJB's cooperative attitude to minimize the need for coercive measures, because in truth they had insufficient forces at their disposal to implement the deportation themselves.

Thus, the AJB functionaries issued the German *Arbeitseinsatz* (work orders) summonses, promising the summoned individuals that the conscription was for labor tasks only. The phrase "compulsory work" was familiar to the Jews: 2,200 had already been sent to work in France to assist in strengthening the Atlantic Wall.*

If only that were true.

In the spirit of the Wannsee Conference,** SS officer Kurt Asche, who was responsible for Jewish affairs in Brussels, received orders to deport 10,000 Jews from Belgium to Auschwitz. On July 27, the Nazis opened the Dossin barracks, a former prison camp, in Mechelen (Malines), located in northern Belgium, as an assembly and transit camp, and the first Jews summoned for "work mobilization" were delivered.

During the summer of 1942, in a frightening sweep of mass arrests throughout Belgium, Jews of foreign nationalities, mostly Polish and German, were rounded up. On Friday night, August 28, 1942, most of the Jews in Antwerp were arrested and deported.

In the hours before dawn came the dreaded pounding on doors. Whole families were roused and given only a moment or two to collect a few belongings. Then, filing out in single column, guided front

---

* The Atlantic Wall was an extensive system of coastal fortifications built by the German Third Reich from 1942 until 1944 along the western coast of Europe to defend against an anticipated British-led Allied invasion of the continent from Great Britain. Thousands of forced laborers were drafted to construct these permanent fortifications along the Dutch, Belgian, and French coasts facing the English Channel (Wikipedia).

** The Wannsee Conference, a meeting of senior officials of the Nazi German regime held in the Berlin suburb of Wannsee on January 20, 1942, was where the "Final Solution to the Jewish Question" was formulated — the systematic plan to exterminate all of European Jewry (Wikipedia).

Left: The memorial plaque mounted on the wall outside the shul, which was dedicated on erev Rosh HaShanah 2000. The plaque reads: "Dedicated to our brethren, men, women, and children, Hy"d, who were pulled from their homes by the Germans on Friday night, 16 Elul, and were brought in trucks to this beis midrash. On that Shabbos, they were deported to the Dossin barracks in Mechelen (Malines) and from there by boxcars to the death camps in Poland, where they suffered until their souls departed."

The Terlist Shul in Antwerp as it appears today

and rear by Gestapo agents, the families were brought to the Terlist Shul, a central shul in the heart of Antwerp. From there they were led away to vans, which transferred them to the primitive barracks at Mechelen.*

Mechelen was nothing less than a torturous waiting room for death. It would be no more than a few days' wait before a train could be filled up — each transport consisting of 1,000 people —

* It was then, at the beginning of the deportation, that the Jewish resistance came to life, known as the Committee for the Defense of Jews — the CDJ. The group, which consisted of various Belgian Jewish and Communist factions, grew on the support of the *Front d'Independence*, the Independence Front, a committee formed in 1941 from various traditional parties in Belgium to preserve the constitutional liberties of the Belgians. The most notable act of resistance occurred on the night of April 19, 1943, when the CDJ derailed a train, leaving the Mechelen detention camp for Auschwitz. Three young students who were members of the CDJ ingeniously fashioned a red lantern using red crepe paper to broadcast the universal danger signal. Seeing the danger warning, the train stopped on the tracks in the middle of a forest between the cities of Boortmeerbeek and Haacht. Despite the security measures of one officer and fifteen Nazi soldiers on board, they were able to open one wagon and liberated 231 people. Of the 231 who managed to jump off the train, 115 successfully escaped. This train was the twentieth of the twenty-eight convoys that transported Jews from Belgium to Auschwitz. This kind of liberating action, today referred to as "The Twentieth Convoy," is unique in the history of the Holocaust — the only documented case of resistance fighters hijacking a death train to free Jews.

to transport them to Auschwitz. From the summer of 1942 until 1944, twenty-eight convoys left Belgium, delivering 25,257 Belgian Jews to Auschwitz. Only 1,221 survived.

With the Nazis' roundups of Jews, the AJB struggled with a brand-new concern: Jewish children who were suddenly and mercilessly turned homeless when they lost their parents during a raid.

Arrival of arrested Jews in the Dossin barracks in Mechelen. Prisoners are ordered to leave their luggage behind. (Photo courtesy of the Jewish Museum of Deportation and Resistance)

In some cases, children returned home from playing or errands, only to be informed by neighbors that their parents had been taken away. Others waited at home alone for days — for parents who never came home, having been nabbed by the Gestapo in the streets. Another group of abandoned Jewish children were those whose parents had hidden them with non-Jewish families in return for financial compensation. When the parents were deported, the funds stopped coming and the "guardian" family turned

The Dossin barracks and the railway tracks after the war. (Photo courtesy of the Jewish Museum of Deportation and Resistance)

the child over to the AJB. And some Jewish children were deposited with the AJB by their parents or relatives for safekeeping. They were either unable to provide for their children any longer — due to the dire economic situation most Jews now faced because of all the oppressive decrees — or they were going into hiding and felt they were unable to take their children with them.

Belgium was predominantly a Catholic country at the time, and the Catholic Church played a pivotal role in Belgium life. During the occupation, many called upon the Catholic Church for protection against Nazi terror and violence. Grappling with the weighty problem of the sizable and steadily increasing group of Jewish children on their hands, the AJB, too, appealed to the Archbishop of Belgium to intervene with the Germans not to deport the children.

They also appealed to the Queen Mother. Queen Elizabeth's intercessions with the German military government were very effective. As many as seven hundred children, despite being registered with the Gestapo, were saved from deportation due to her efforts.*

In the spring of 1943, a historically obscure German policy was instituted that proved a salvation for the very young and old. Jews who were unfit for work — children under the age of sixteen and the elderly — would not be deported. Instead, the Nazis allowed them to seek shelter in AJB-maintained orphanages and senior homes.

The Nazis saving old people and children? What lay behind this sudden magnanimity?

The Nazis' authorization of the establishment of AJB-managed public homes for the very young and aged of Belgium was nothing short of a diabolical act of psychological warfare. In nearly every one of the Eastern European countries that the Nazis occupied, the local gentile population were all too willing and gleeful accomplices to the Nazis' "Final Solution." The Belgian population, however, did not have an extreme record of anti-Semitism. After the deportations began in earnest

* Later Yad Vashem acknowledged Queen Elizabeth as one of the righteous among the nations.

in 1942, the Nazis had to concern themselves with a growing resistance movement that had sprung up in defiance of their actions and the public opinion that decried the sadistic treatment of their fellow citizens. The Nazis conspired that if they could somehow keep the Belgian population — Jewish and non-Jewish — unaware of the real reason for deportation, they could avert open objection from the non-Jewish population and the Belgian authorities and keep the Jews from undertaking active resistance or flight.

"We cannot understand it," said one of the AJB directors after an SS officer, in the course of making an inspection of a new Jewish home for the elderly, indicated that he cared for the comfort of the residents.*

This was the lie the Nazis perpetrated: that Jews were being deported for labor and resettlement in the East. By openly authorizing the establishment of residential institutions — the AJB homes for orphaned children and for the elderly — the Nazis attempted to lend some credence to their ruse. After all, sending the children and the elderly to labor camps would be inconsistent with such a representation. Moreover, they could contain the children and elderly in their own lairs — the homes they had created — where they would be easy targets for deportation when the time was ripe.

The Germans also hoped to lure Jews already in hiding to seek protection against deportation by seeking employment in these homes — more Jews for the Nazis to dispose of when the time came.

And so this drama began playing itself out. The AJB assumed control of various old-age homes, hospitals, and orphanages in Belgium. Many were wary and apprehensive about these "protected sanctuaries"; in some of the old-age homes, the directors insisted that the residents sign release papers to absolve the AJB of responsibility in case of Nazi roundups.

Hundreds of children were released from the Malines detention camp and handed over to the AJB homes. On April 14, 1943, nine

* See *Belgium and the Holocaust,* 359, quoting from the *Van Der Berg War Diary*, op. cit., August 25, 1943, 111.

months after the first street raids against the Jews, the secretary general of the Ministry of Justice, Gaston Schuind, wrote a letter to the German military counselor, Frank Thediek, the personal representative of the German military administration. Schuind requested the release of three hundred children under the age of sixteen and some elderly people who were scheduled for deportation. He reminded Thediek that the German authorities had agreed to "the establishment of institutions to take in children in need" — that is, abandoned children. Consequently, 365 Jewish children and seniors were released from Malines and sent to AJB homes.*

When the AJB began parceling out the war orphans the Gestapo had sent them among the Belgian Jewish orphanages, the AJB assumed official responsibility for the Tiefenbrunner Home. Because Nazi oppression toward Jews was strongest in Antwerp in all of Belgium, the Tiefenbrunners had moved their home to Brussels in the beginning of 1942. They now occupied a pretty townhouse at 34 Rue des Patriotes. Their official name was *Orphelinat Israelite de Bruxelles* (The Jewish Orphanage of Brussels), but it was affectionately known as *Chez Tiefenbrunner* (the Tiefenbrunner Home).

Thus the Tiefenbrunners' home became one of the seven orphanages in Belgium that were eventually operated by the AJB under the German occupation.** The orphanages were given quite a bit of leeway in terms of internal management and the education of their wards. The AJB provided food and clothing for the children, and materials for the maintenance and operation of the physical premises. Thus, with the AJB's acquisition of his home, Yona's financial burden was eased.

Of all the orphanages, the Tiefenbrunner Home had two important distinctions. It was the only one that was directed by religious Jews and run completely according to Torah principles. And it was the only orphanage that was never referred to by its official name, but rather as simply, "the Tiefenbrunner Home."

When one realizes to what extent Yona devoted himself to "his" children, it is little wonder that the surviving children never refer to it

---

* See *Belgium and the Holocaust*, 422.

** The other orphanages were the *Joodsch Weeshhuis*, the Linkebeek Home, the Home De La-Bas, the Wezembeek Home, and the nurseries in Uccle and Etterbeek.

as the "AJB orphanage." Yona and Ruth's home was no more than a religious home with a big family who welcomed each newcomer with open arms and hearts.

And so began the saga of countless children and staff members saved from deportation by Yona and Ruth Tiefenbrunner, who took all these souls into their home during those terrible times.

4
New Arrivals

Abruptly shattered childhoods. Fear of the unknown. Weighty burdens of personal sorrow and grief. Perhaps this was all that the disparate group of arrivals — boys and girls ranging in age from four to fifteen — shared upon crossing the threshold of 34 Rue des Patriotes between 1942 and 1944. Little could they dream that soon enough Yona would succeed in making them all feel like brothers and sisters in one large family in this warm haven from the maelstrom outside.

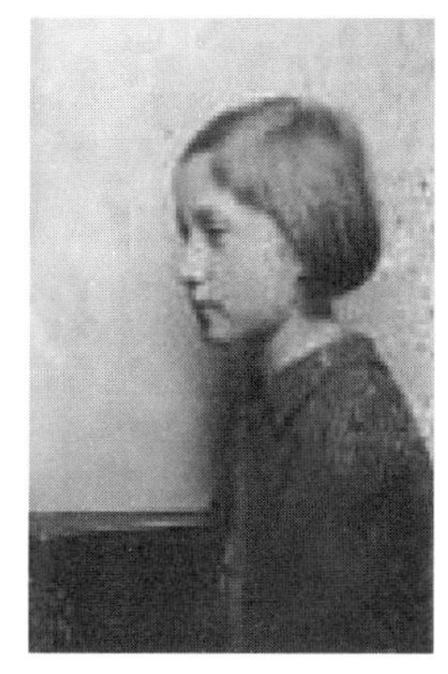

Identity photos taken upon arrival at the Tiefenbrunner Home, 1942–44

The first impressions for many arriving children was of a surrealistic scene. The world they had inhabited until now was characterized by the ever-present fear of impending arrest. The people they knew wore grim, drawn faces and whispered anxiously of escape. Their world was a place where friends, relatives — even parents — disappeared without warning, never to be seen or heard from again.

But upon entering the home, these frightened children saw something they had not seen for a long time: friendly faces. A young authoritative but kind-looking man wearing a large yarmulke greeted them. He was surrounded by dozens of religious children seated in a well-appointed dining room eating kosher food. The atmosphere was of blissful calm, seemingly impervious to the fear that reigned outside.

This is the scene that greeted Sarah,* who arrived at the home in 1943. Her parents, who lived in Antwerp, had hidden her with gentiles in return for payment. When her parents were deported, the payment stopped coming and the gentile woman no longer wanted to care for her. Grabbing her by the hand, she led Sarah out of her house one day, taking her to a nondescript house on Rue des Patriotes. She knocked firmly and, when the door opened, asked to see the director immediately.

"See this child?" she said to Yona. "She's Jewish. Either you take her off my hands now, or I will drop her off at the Gestapo!"

"We were very happy children," Sarah recalls. "There was laughter, there was music — we were given piano lessons, and the talented girls would often play. There was orderliness, and we were taught to be exceptionally well mannered. Only after we had grown up and moved out into real life did we sense that we were orphans — that we had no family."**

It was no small feat to generate this island of tranquility amid the backdrop of a raging war. The Tiefenbrunners sacrificed the most beautiful years of their young marriage to the maintenance — both spiritual and physical — of the home.

The outer façade of number 34 was similar to the other houses on the

---

* Not her real name.

** Sarah lived in the home for eleven years until her marriage in 1954. Yona and Ruth Tiefenbrunner walked her to her *chuppah*. Today she is the grandmother of a large beautiful family. She says that she is religious, that her children and grandchildren are religious, only because of Mr. Tiefenbrunner.

street. It was a large private house. The white marbled main entrance was reserved for important visitors. The children used the basement door on the left of the house, which led to the coatroom. Next to it was the kitchen. Dark wooden stairs led to the ground level, where the office and the double dining room — whose walls were adorned with murals of classic children's storybook characters — were located. The dining room doubled as a classroom.

34 Rue des Patriotes, the Tiefenbrunner Home

The children were grouped according to age. Each group had its own name, room, and supervising counselor. The Tiefenbrunners' bedroom was located on the first floor, along with two bedrooms for the younger boys and the infirmary. The girls slept in two bedrooms on the second floor, and the older boys' quarters were on the third.

On the roof of the Tiefenbrunner Home. The photo was taken sometime between 1942 and 1943

In the backyard of the Tiefenbrunner Home

After concerning himself with providing for the children's physical needs, Yona's first order of business was to see to their education. The expulsion of Jewish children from public school precluded them from attending the local school (a heretofore accepted practice), so he set about organizing a curriculum in the house.

Seligman Bamberger, 1944

Yona himself would teach *limudei kodesh*, aided by Mr. Seligman Bamberger, a recently married young man, who came every day to the home with his wife, Rosa. This was the start of the deep and enduring friendship between the Tiefenbrunner and Bamberger families, the two young couples bound together by bravery and devotion.*

The basic Jewish studies curriculum included reading and writing, *lashon hakodesh*, *tefillah* (learning how to daven from a siddur and the meaning of the prayers), and *Yahadus* (religion). The older students also studied *Chumash* with *Rashi*, *dikduk* (Hebrew grammar), and Jewish history.

For general knowledge subjects, the older children, among them Steffie Wieruszawski and Nathan Kirschbaum, taught the younger ones. Then Yona recruited Jewish teachers, some of whom had been university professors before they were fired from their jobs for being Jewish. (In addition to expelling Jews from teaching positions, the law also forbade non-Jews from teaching Jewish children.) Miss Miriam Neuberger taught the little children; Miss Chana Perelman, middle-school age. The older students studied in the basement under the leadership of Mr. Katzenellenbogen. The curriculum included French and Flemish, arithmetic, history, geography, sciences, drawing, music, hygiene, and gymnastics.

In addition to the teachers, the staff members included the pediatrician, Dr. Sperka; the dentist, Herbert Wilde; the cook, Ruchla Szezy-

---

* Selig Bamberger's niece, Miriam Weinstein (now Bamberger), was one the new arrivals at the home. "I was fourteen years old when I was separated from my mother and brother," she says. "My father had been taken two years earlier. For two months I was hidden by a gentile family, until I learned that someone had betrayed my whereabouts. I escaped in the nick of time. I returned to my home, where I learned that the Gestapo had taken my mother and brother. Some neighbors informed me that my uncle, Selig Bamberger, was working in a children's home. They phoned him, asking him to come for me, because my hiding place had not worked out. Mr. Tiefenbrunner accepted me with warmth and love, and his home became my second home."

gielska; and the counselors, Gila Hirsz, Paula Klein, Nini Brinkman, Rosa Hartman, Laja Cwajsfuss, Lucienne Polak, Sonia Dreispiel-Hiller, and Helen Auslander.

A staff member wearing the yellow star, 1942

The staff came and went through the war years, some eventually escaping with the help of the resistance movement. For the most part, the staff members employed by the AJB-sponsored orphanage lived outside the home, coming daily or as needed. The Gestapo issued legal working papers to the adults who worked in their sanctioned children's homes. Aware that every additional set of working papers could buy another adult's safety from deportation, Yona constantly submitted applications to the Gestapo for the maximum amount of staff members, making every effort to save as many as he could. In one instance, a young woman approached him for a job. Having no spare working papers, Yona personally arranged work for her in another orphanage.

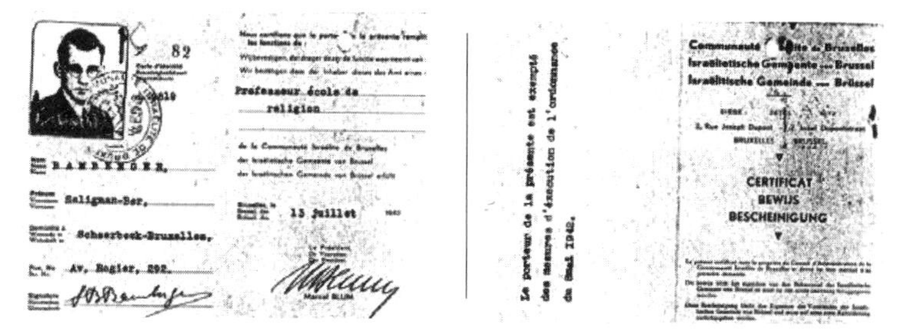

82

BAMBERGER,

Seligman-Ber,

Schaerbeek-Bruxelles,

Av. Rogier, 292.

Professeur école de religion

13 Juillet

Marcel BLUM

Le porteur de la présente est exempté des mesures d'exécution de l'ordonnance du 8mai 1942.

Communauté Israélite de Bruxelles
Israëlietische Gemeente — Brussel
Israëlitische Gemeinde — Brüssel

CERTIFICAT
BEWIJS
BESCHEINIGUNG

Certificate issued by the AJB in Brussels on July 13, 1942, confirming the position of Seligman Bamberger as a teacher of religion. On the back of this card: "The holder of this card is not submitted to the law of May 8, 1942 [against the Jews]."

The days were hectic for "the Director," who was literally occupied from morning till night. A typical day might have unfolded like this:

Yona rose early to light the boilers for heat. Then he joined the children for the *shacharis* prayers, the start of their day. After supervising breakfast and arranging the day's curriculum, he would leave for City Hall to pick up food-ration cards, and then meet with members of the AJB or the CDJ (Committee for the Defense of Jews, the underground Belgian Jewish resistance movement who helped people escape). When he completed his meetings, he would rush back home. The children were waiting for him! He knew how eagerly the children anticipated his return, hungry for his fatherly love, his listening ear and heart.

After spending some casual time with the children, patting one on the back, listening somberly to another child's complaint and promising to rectify it, and taking a private walk with a third who needed the individual attention, Yona would sit down to his paperwork. Then it was bedtime, and he would accompany his little troop to bed with pleasant good-night wishes and the timeless words of Shema.

And as surely as "Monsieur," as Yona Tiefenbrunner was loving addressed by the children, was always there for them, so was "Madame" — Ruth Tiefenbrunner, the consummate *eishes chayil*, ever present at his side. With her more reserved persona, the newly married Ruth could have insisted on living a more private life with her husband to raise the three children they would have. But this young woman of valor did not seek a life of entitlement. Like Ruth of the Torah and her famous utterance, "Where you go, I will go," she dutifully followed her husband's calling, cooking, cleaning, and caring for all the children who came into their home. Pregnant with her first child, Ruth's legs were often swollen from the hours spent standing on her feet in the kitchen and mopping the three flights of stairs, going up, going down, and going up again.

She did her utmost to lend a semblance of normalcy to the children's lives. In addition to her regular household duties, one evening a week Madame would gather all the girls together in a sewing circle, and they would mend torn stockings and clothing and even do some embroidery.

"Mrs. Tiefenbrunner was a true *eizer kenegdo*," recalls Rachel Kirschbaum-Schwartz. "Today, as a mother of a family, I have a much clearer understanding of the extent of her sacrifice. They were a young couple who could have escaped, but instead chose to jeopardize their safety in order to save a houseful of Jewish orphans."

Yona and Ruth Tiefenbrunner with their daughter Jeannette, four months old

In December of 1942, Ruth gave birth to their eldest daughter, Jeannette.* Some months later, in June, Seligman and Rosa Bamberger were also blessed with their first child, a son named Moishe.

Two young mothers, each blessed with the precious gift of new life! But their distrust of the Nazis, and the pervasive fear of deportation hovering over them, compelled Ruth, thirty-two years old at the time, and Rosa, only twenty-two, to make a heartrending decision: they would place babies Jeannette and Moishe in a non-Jewish nursery under fictitious gentile names. If they were arrested and deported, they reasoned, at least their babies would live.

Ruth tattooed an identifying symbol on six-month-old Jeannette's chest before handing her over to a nursery that was housed in a Catholic convent. Sometimes Ruth managed to sneak into the nursery, disguised as a visiting nurse, to see her baby.

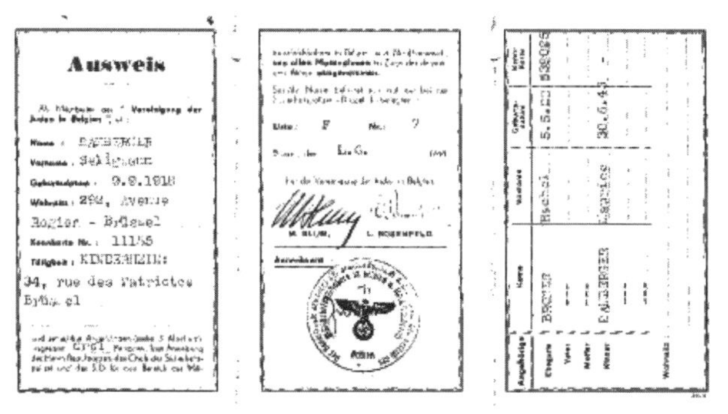

Ausweis

34, rue des Patriotes

M. BLUM, L. ROSENFELD

Identity cards issued by the AJB in Brussels for Rachel (Rosa) Bamberger and her son, Moishe (Maurice) Bamberger, 1944

---

* They would have two more daughters: Judith, in 1945, and Mariette, in 1948.

Ruth and Rosa constantly grappled with their decision. To have faith in Hashem and take the babies back, or allow them to grow into toddlerhood under the pernicious influence of the church?

In any case, six months later, when Jeannette was just turning a year old, the disquieting dilemma was resolved. The nursery informed them that they could no longer keep the children. Jeannette and Moishe were brought home, where they were tearfully embraced by their parents, the bittersweet reality mixed with gratitude at having the children home and tinged with a prayer that their young innocent offspring be granted life during those terrible days.

5
One Large Family

Living at 34 Rue des Patriotes was like living in a large family. A large family, indeed: at its peak, there were forty children living in the home!

It was Yona who turned them into one family. He had created the bonds of brotherliness between the children, imparting to them a sense of normalcy and responsibility for one another. The older ones — the thirteen- to fifteen-year-olds — cared for the younger children, treating them as kid sisters and brothers. And, as in all large families, the older children helped with the housekeeping and maintenance.

Steffie Wieruszawski was in charge of setting the tables and serving the meals. Kurt Dressler helped in the infirmary and was Yona's personal secretary. Miriam Gelbart was in charge of the laundry, and Jeff Ajdler was the "handyman," in charge of household repairs and running errands in town.

Herbert Kessler, one of the oldest children, was the "Minister of Foreign Affairs," as his "brothers" and "sisters" affectionately nicknamed him. He was often assigned to outside missions. His attaché case clutched tightly to his chest in an attempt to cover the coat lapel bearing the incriminating yellow star, and a letter in his pocket certifying that he was working for the orphanage, he would brave the streets of

Brussels, hurrying to his destination. Sometimes he would go to obtain food supplies, such as meat, fruit, sweets, and biscuits, from the Winter Aid Group, a child health-care program created by the Germans, which proffered food subsidies and extra ration cards for children and, oddly enough, included the AJB homes in their distribution. Other times, he was sent to retrieve money from wealthy Jews, among them Fishel Ferdman, chairman of the AJB.

During these terrible times, the Tiefenbrunner Home, in addition to offering physical shelter, provided enormous emotional support to the children, the rainbow of color behind the gray clouds. Kindness, warmth, and camaraderie mitigated the overwhelming sensations of bereavement and loss.

Doing laundry in the backyard of the home, 1942

Very quickly the children grew to adore and respect Yona, who was truly more father than principal to them. Despite his daunting schedule, he always carved out time to listen to their personal problems, to be their confidant. He would kibbitz and tease them, too, and, possessed of a strong physique, Yona would occasionally wrestle playfully with the older boys.

Rarely would Yona need to dispense the punishment of a slap on the wrist, and only when the crime would truly endanger the child or other children. Joseph* remembers that during the bombings everyone was ordered to go down to the basement, but he was curious and stayed upstairs to look out the windows. He ignored Yona's second request for him to go downstairs. Yona picked him up and carried him down the stairs, whereupon he slapped him on the hand.

"He only slapped me to impress upon me the extent of the danger. I know this because shortly afterward I saw him crying, upset that he had to hit me."

* Name has been changed.

Yona never imposed himself on the children. His authority emanated from his personality, a composite of an innate sense of fairness and kindness. It wasn't unusual for Yona to come into the kitchen and join the children in peeling potatoes for dinner. Potato and peeler in hand, he would listen to their stories and regale them with fascinating stories of his own.

The children were, for the most part, rather carefree. Giggles and quibbles, laughter and pranks, the usual stuff of childhood, were part of growing up in the home that strove mightily to shut out the war.

Like a doting parent, Yona worked hard to incorporate pleasant childhood pastimes for his children. The neighbors on Rue des Patriotes would often observe orderly groups of Jewish children — yellow stars and all — merrily making their way down the street, with carefree abandon. Their destination? The local public park for hours of play and physical activity. Summertime, they would take the tram to Auderghem, a rural area in the outskirts of Brussels. The freedom and expanse of the pastoral settings were indeed tonic for their spirits, as they would hike their way through green fields, marching and singing animatedly. Favorite activities there were ball playing and berry picking.

They even had birthday parties, like the one Maurice Krollick recalls. Maurice was the first child to arrive, at the age of nine, to the Tiefenbrunner Home in late 1940. Maurice had already been away from his parents for over two years. He had been born in Berlin, Germany, and after Kristallnacht his parents smuggled him out of Germany to Belgium. Maurice had spent some time in a non-Jewish orphanage before his aunt, who was living in Antwerp, found him and took him into her home. But due to the financial hardships created by the Nazi occupation, she could not support him for long. She learned of the Tiefenbrunner Home from a local rabbi. She asked Maurice to write a letter asking to be accepted.

Maurice Krollick's identity photo, taken upon his arrival at the Tiefenbrunner Home, 1940

Maurice was the first of the young children to arrive in the home. Until then it had been only for teenagers. At first, he was afraid of everything. He missed his parents, whom he hadn't heard from, and he had a gut feeling that he had lost his family forever. He was so nervous, so emotionally stressed out, that he had developed a facial tic. Mr. Tiefenbrunner's responsibilities were daunting, but he carved out time — five minutes or ten now and then — to walk with the boy in the garden to calm him. Eventually, he succeeded in knocking out the disfiguring habit from the boy's psyche.

For his eleventh birthday, Maurice's "older siblings" surprised him with several birthday presents: two pears and two apples — precious gifts, given the severely rationed food supply — along with a pair of socks that Sophie, three years his senior, had surreptitiously knitted for him out of old wool scraps.*

Caring for the basic physical needs of the children was a greater challenge. Among the universal catastrophes the war had wreaked was the problem of food shortages, and the Tiefenbrunner Home was, of course, affected. Though the AJB did supply food, some of the older boys didn't have enough to eat. With anti-*shechitah* laws in effect since 1940, no ritually slaughtered meat was obtainable. Beets often constituted the main part of the day's menu, leaving the older children — teenagers in their growing years — hungry. Some days the bread supply was limited and the slices had to be cut very thinly. Each child would receive two thin slices smeared with artificial honey, with the children vying for the thickest slices.

Food was a main topic in the bedtime chatter of the younger children, each weighing in on the hotly debated subject of "who is stealing all the food?!" But the older ones never complained. They knew that Monsieur Tiefenbrunner never left a rock unturned to obtain food — a handful of onions, a couple of extra potatoes, anything he could scrounge up.

Some of the counselors dipped into their meager salaries to purchase

* Maurice spent seven years in the home, until his emigration to America in 1947, at the age of sixteen. He lives there still, in New York, and works as an attorney. "Throughout my stay," he says, "Mr. Tiefenbrunner remained attentive to my individual needs. After the war, I was the only one who remained a student, while all the others had already begun working. Mr. Tiefenbrunner read me so well — he recognized my great learning potential and persuaded me to continue studying."

bread and fruit for the children on the black market. The older children who had some pocket money (from doing tasks in the home or from a relative) would purchase whatever bread they could. Mr. Tiefenbrunner, noticing the extra bread, would ask the boys where it came from, wanting to ascertain that it had been procured through honest means.

But even for money, there was little food to be gotten. And with the absence of meat and poultry in their diets, a number of children manifested signs of malnutrition. Dr. Sperka, the attending pediatrician, recommended that the small children be given meat twice a week. Yona sought halachic counsel from Rabbi Lowy (one of the two *rabbanim* in hiding who frequented the Tiefenbrunner Home's Shabbos minyan).* He determined that the smallest and weakest children could receive nonkosher meat under specific circumstances. He advised Yona to *kasher* this meat as if it were meat provided from ritual *shechitah*, and so the meat was soaked in water and salted to remove the blood and given a final rinsing before cooking.

Yona obtained separate pots for Ruth to cook the meat in, in a separate corner of the kitchen, and the children ate their portions in the cellar in small groups. Years later Ruth Tiefenbrunner would recount the challenge of smelling the tempting aromas wafting out of the pots of meat she cooked and prepared, yet never tasting a morsel herself, despite the prevailing conditions.

"Disinfection" was another issue to contend with. Concern about the spreading of contagious diseases bred by malnutrition led the Belgian Health Department to mandate periodic disinfection routines for all Belgian children.

The younger children were agitated about this new regulation and put up a fuss. To undress in front of strange health officials, and further be humiliated by being sprayed with foul-smelling disinfectant sprays? They all knew that hygiene was strictly enforced in the home and they were free of lice and fleas. Why did they need to go through this aggravation?

Yona didn't spend time on superfluous words.

"I'm going with you," he said, even though the disinfection was mandated only for children, not adults. "I'll be disinfected first, and

* Rabbi Lowy survived the war and now lives in Israel.

you'll see there's nothing to fear."

The children quieted down and followed him without further complaint. If Monsieur could be disinfected, so could they.

Just as Yona sustained the children physically and emotionally, he accepted the full responsibility of seeing to the spiritual needs of "his" children, embracing his role as a surrogate father. From its inception, the Tiefenbrunner Home was grounded in Torah ideals and tradition.

Every morning began with davening. The bar mitzvah boys donned tefillin. *Berachos* were recited before eating, and every meal concluded with Birkas HaMazon recited aloud. Every child was taught about Hashem, to open their eyes in the morning and thank Him with "*Modeh Ani*," to end their day with Shema at bedtime.

If every day was special, Shabbos and *yom tov* were the highlights, days that positively glowed with the holiness and reverence that Yona attached to them. Shabbos meant a white shirt for every boy, which Yona somehow managed to procure. There was a weekly Shabbos minyan at the Tiefenbrunner Home, with the participation of some people from the outside, among them Rabbi Feuerwerker and Rabbi Lowy, two *rabbanim* in hiding.

After davening, the children would line up in front of Monsieur Tiefenbrunner for the time-worn custom of blessing one's children on Friday night. He would place his hands on the head of each and every one and bless them, one at a time. The healing sensations of this weekly touch of kindness would be forever etched in the minds of the children.

After the children received a piece of the "*motzi*," the challah dipped in salt, Monsieur would discuss the parashah of the week. *Zemiros* were sung at every meal. Many children vividly recall the *seudah shelishis*, when Yona's voice resonated passionately in the darkened room with the soulful "*Mizmor L'David Hashem Ro'i Lo Echsar*" (A psalm to David, G-d is My shepherd; I shall not want), a poignant message of hope and faith during those dark times.

Round the year, the *yamim tovim* abounded with opportunities to

Purim at 34 Rue des Patriotes, 1942

share love as well as *mesorah*. For Sukkos, to the delight and fascination of the children, they built a sukkah in the backyard, where they would have their *yom tov* meals, rich in spirit if not in fare. On Chanukah the menorah was lit, and the children prepared presents for their friends. When Purim came around, great pains were taken to outfit the children in costumes, to celebrate this day of happiness and festivity in the traditional way. And who can forget the hilarious Purim plays the older children performed, eliciting much mirth and laughter?

The children and staff prepared for Pesach with great enthusiasm. All the children participated in the Pesach cleaning. One of the more exciting tasks was *kashering* all the dishes and cutlery. It was great fun — a change from the ordinary routine — for each child to carry what they could to the yard to be immersed in big vats filled with boiling water. It signified the imminent arrival of the long-awaited *chag*. And in addition to receiving matzos from the Parein Factory (a Belgian biscuit factory), baked under the supervision of Rabbi Ullman, the Tiefenbrunner children would bake their own matzos in a special matzah oven in the cellar of the home. At the Pesach Seder, every child was given the chance to recite the *Mah Nishtanah*. Replete with symbols of hope and freedom — much-needed messages in those times — the Seder lasted till deep into the night.

Bar mitzvahs in the Tiefenbrunner home were bittersweet occa-

Kurt Dressler, zt"l, celebrating his bar mitzvah, 1941

sions. The most awaited milestone of every adolescent Jewish boy was overshadowed by the black grief, always present but not necessarily articulated, that their beloved parents and family members weren't with them to share their momentous occasion.

Some believed the illusion the Nazis perpetuated that their parents had only gone to "work" in a labor camp and would return after the war. Others knew the brutal truth, having witnessed their parents' murders. In either case, Yona, the father of orphans, was there for them. Although Yona had no biological sons, he hosted many bar mitzvahs during the war years. Each party was understandably a modest affair, the best possible under wartime conditions, but unforgettable in the memory banks of these boys. Yona painstakingly taught each one how to lay tefillin, and arranged lessons for them to learn the *leining* so they could read their bar mitzvah parashah on Shabbos.

Beloved, dedicated, Yona was truly G-d-sent, a divinely chosen emissary to assist and sustain them in every way, physically, emotionally, and spiritually.

6

Facing the Monster: Gestapo Visits

"*Aufmachen*! (Open up!)"

The children are rudely awakened, their eyes wide with fear, to the cacophony of ear-splitting noise piercing the midnight silence. The doorbell is ringing, accompanied by coarse German shouts, but before anyone can get to the door, the pounding rifle butts have broken it down. In burst the notorious *Feldgendarmerie,* the Nazi military police.

From room to room they stride, illuminating the thick darkness* with the harsh glare of their flashlights. Everywhere, they cast threatening shadows. In every corner. Under every bed. In every closet. And finally, one by one, upon the face of every terrified youngster.

"How can you pretend this boy is not seventeen?" they thunder scornfully. Their flashlights are fixed on Herbert Kessler, who has an exceptionally tall build so that his feet protrude from the end of the bed.

"Get up now!"

"I've known his family since he was a baby. He is only fourteen,

* They were forbidden from turning on any lights during the evening curfew hours.

though he looks older," argues the room counselor, Helen, with a bravery that is characteristic of many of the wartime staff members. "You well know that we don't keep grown-up children here. Now why are you taking children out of bed in the middle of the night?"

Helen apparently succeeds in convincing the Germans this time. Wordlessly, they file out.

It was all too often that the Gestapo dispatched the Nazi military police for periodic raids on the Tiefenbrunner Home to ascertain that the orphanage was not sheltering any unauthorized persons — no children above age 16, nor any adults who weren't staff members. The sudden nighttime raids were part of their ruse to instill fear and panic so that the discombobulated children might disclose their real ages.

Sometimes they would gather only the older children, ordering them to stand in a circle so they could size them up and interrogate them. Moshe, a tall teenager who had just turned sixteen, was slightly learning disabled and socially impaired. Again and again his "brothers" drilled it in: "When the Nazis come, say you're fifteen!" How they cowered in fear, attempting to keep their knees from quivering, each time they questioned Moshe lest he mumble the wrong answer. Thankfully, he was never taken and survived the war.

There were numerous instances of Divine Providence that protected Yona and his charges. One evening, a German officer and his soldiers stormed into the home, ordering all the children out so they could search the house. Yona began arguing with the officer in German, telling him that it was impossible, given the unearthly hour.

The officer whirled around to face Yona, his face inexplicably taking on a humane hue.

"Where are you from?" he mumbled, taken aback by Yona's German accent.

"From Wiesbaden, sir."

"Wiesbaden! I, too, grew up in Wiesbaden!"

The officer questioned Yona further and realized that they had both attended the same public school years, nay, a lifetime ago. Lost in the shared pleasant reveries of their youth, the officer politely wished Yona good night and left with his cohorts.

Late one evening, Yona heard a desperate knocking on the door.

"Please hide me!" came a cry. The hapless Jew pushed his way in. "The Nazis are chasing me!"

To shelter an adult was to jeopardize the entire home. No adults, save for those officially employed by the AJB to work in the home, were allowed here. But Yona's deeply honed sense of compassion overtook him.

"Hide in the attic!" he said. Within seconds the man had disappeared into the dark attic that was used for storage.

It was none too soon. Another furious pounding on the door, this time accompanied by rifle butts and kicks.

"Where is that Jew?" the Gestapo soldiers spat out.

"He isn't here," replied Yona evenly. "No adults are in this home."

They tore past him, searching every corner of the house. When they reached the windowless attic, it was pitch-dark. Night had fallen. Stumbling along the nearest wall, they were feeling for the light switch to illuminate the space piled high with all manner of boxes, crates, trunks, and old furniture.

The light did not go on. No amount of fumbling could make it turn on. There was no way to navigate the attic in the thick, blinding darkness. With curses on their breaths, they turned around and left.

When the coast was clear, Yona wondered: how could the Jew have escaped the windowless attic? Running up the stairs, he entered the attic and flicked on the light switch. Light flooded the room.

"They're gone! You can come out of hiding now!" announced Yona.

A trunk creaked open, and the man slowly rose, shaking from witnessing the open miracle of the on-again-off-again lightbulb that had assisted Yona in saving one more.

Time and again, Yona manifested unimaginable reserves of *mesiras nefesh*, leaving no stone unturned when it came to trying to save even one person. Herbert Kessler recalls the time Yona went straight into the lion's den, the Gestapo headquarters, demanding the release of a child with the dire knowledge that that they could easily shoot him on the spot for his insolence.

"Once, on Shabbos morning during davening, Mr. Tiefenbrunner approached me and said, 'Herbert, take off your tallis and come with me.' We left the house, heading straight to the tram. I was astounded. Traveling on Shabbos? Confused, I asked Mr. Tiefenbrunner what happened. How did it come to be that he was traveling on Shabbos? On the way, he told me that he had just learned that the Gestapo was holding a boy they were ready to free. There was no time to lose because they could change their minds at any moment.

" 'I want to try to get this boy out of there,' Yona told me. 'I will tell them I'm not leaving without the boy. But I want you to come with me so that if something happens to me, you will report back to the home, informing them that I won't be coming back.' When we reached the Gestapo headquarters at Avenue Louise, he told me to wait at the street corner. From there the entrance of the Gestapo headquarters was clearly visible.

" 'Keep checking to see if they take us away in a car. Wait exactly half an hour.' He handed me his gold watch so that I could keep track of the time. 'If I don't come back with the child, return as quickly as you can to the home and tell them to disperse all the children within two hours. Maybe I will return later, so somebody should stay and watch the house. Send the children to play in the Square Margueritte, but don't tell them anything. If I do not come back, advise Blum (a senior staff member in the home) that I have been arrested and that everyone should run and hide since they will come after everyone in the home as well.'

"He entered the Gestapo headquarters, and I waited at the corner with his watch in my hand, my eyes peeled on the entrance. I waited and waited... I don't think that in my life I have ever experienced such a long half-hour!

"At the last minute he came out with the child, white as a sheet. He shook my hand, and we returned to the home. The morning prayers were over, and he didn't mention a word about what had happened. But the next Friday night, when it was my turn to receive his weekly blessing, his hand rested a little longer on my head, and he shook my hand with more strength than usual as he greeted me with '*Gut Shabbos*.'"

On another occasion, the Nazis broke the door down with their rifle butts after pounding on the door and stormed in. This time, they simply grabbed Yona and took him back to the Gestapo headquarters for questioning.

They were looking for a particular staff member who had once been employed in the home. Yona had asked her to leave since she had become active in a Communist resistance organization, and Yona, aware that the communists were enemies of the Nazis, felt her presence would endanger the home. A friend of this girl had been arrested and under torture had given this girl's name and her address — the Tiefenbrunner Home.

The Gestapo demanded that Yona reveal her whereabouts. He told them she had left the institution and he had had no further contact with her. The interrogating officer didn't believe him, of course, and brought him into the basement, ordering Yona to face the wall.

"I'm counting to ten!" snarled the SS officer. "If you don't reveal her whereabouts by the count of ten, you will be shot!"

Two SS men were stationed behind the officer, their guns pointing to Yona's back.

The countdown began. Yona remained stoically silent. He was telling the truth: he had no answers to provide because he did not know where she was. But it was safe to say that even under the threat of certain death, as evidenced on so many other occasions, Yona would not have caused hurt to another Jew.

The courage of his convictions was stronger than fear. This extraordinary man of character and nobility never regarded himself as a hero. He believed himself to be an ordinary individual who did what he believed any humane, compassionate person would have done in similar circumstances because doing anything else was inconceivable.

"Ten!" barked the SS officer. And "Fire!" he ordered his men, fully expecting Yona to turn around and plead for mercy. But Yona never wavered.

The SS men withdrew their guns, which in any case weren't loaded. It had all been a ploy from the start. Knowing that they couldn't tamper with the director of the AJB-approved and Gestapo-registered children's institution, they had concocted this setup with the intent of scaring Yona into submission. But, of course, they had underestimated their target.

Bessi Mittelman (née Sturm) remembers the fateful evening she lay in bed quaking with fear. There was a ruckus going on downstairs...

"*Shturm, Bessi und Harry! Wo sind diese Kinder? Geben Sie sie uns schnell!*" (Where are these children? Give them to us, quickly!) German voices roared, the cruel words puncturing the evening stillness and striking terror in her heart.

Having spent her first eight years growing up in Vienna, Bessi could clearly understand the German orders. It was the lives of her and her little brother that those Germans were after!

Bessi had been eight years old when her father, her stepmother (her own mother had passed away in childbirth, when Harry was born), she, and her little brother, Harry, fled Vienna in early 1940, seeking refuge from the Nazis in neutral Belgium. When the Nazis invaded Belgium, she remembers joining the thousands fleeing to France, encountering abandoned farmhouses along the way, with the unforgettable stench of animal carcasses, only to turn around and return to Antwerp because there was no refuge in Nazi-occupied France either.

In 1942, upon receiving the summons for "work mobilization" — the dreaded deportation order — her father had placed her, then age 12, and six-year-old Harry in the Tiefenbrunner Home for safekeeping until he could return for them. Her stepmother went into hiding with a gentile family, and periodically she would sneak out to visit the two children.

The dreaded day came when the Gestapo arrested Bessi's stepmother — they had followed her to the orphanage! And now, two Gestapo agents had burst through the front door and were roughly barking out orders to the director to hand over Bessi and Harry!

Bessi sucked in her breath, screwed her eyes tightly shut. The other children had awakened, too, and their eyes were wide with terror. They couldn't see the confidence that the typically unassuming Yona exuded, his feet planted firmly on the floor in front of him, his posture ramrod straight, his arms folded authoritatively across his chest. But they could hear him launching into yet another one of his verbal counteroffenses as he battled for the two helpless orphans in his care.

"Don't waste your time coming here," he chastised them in flawless German. "You know Gestapo headquarters have authorized the establishment of this home for children under sixteen. These children are thirteen and seven. They have been here for over a year, practically since our inception."

It was not an invincible argument; the Nazis' establishment of the orphanages was merely a pretext to cover up the wholesale annihilation of Belgium's Jews. The token children they sheltered in the officially sanctioned homes did not preclude them from deporting children at whim.

But Yona had succeeded in persuading the Gestapo agents to leave the children alone, and they left.

When Bessi heard the door close behind them, she broke into tears of relief. Later Bessi learned that both her father and her stepmother had been gassed in Auschwitz. Now, when Bessi considers her six children, twenty-two grandchildren, and twenty-seven great-grandchildren, she knows that Yona envisioned these generations, too, when he put his life on the line for her.

Not all encounters with the Nazis ended so well.

One day, some Jewish families were arrested in a restaurant in Brussels. The men were taken into the Gestapo headquarters, while the women and children were placed temporarily in the Tiefenbrunner Home. The women were very distressed at being separated from their husbands. Several days later, the women were informed that they could join their husbands in Malines (Mechelen), the Belgian concentration camp. Yona and Ruth pleaded with them to at least leave the children with them, but they refused. All were deported from Malines to Auschwitz and gassed, save for one child, who had been hospitalized in Brussels for appendicitis and then returned to the Tiefenbrunner Home.

Once, the Germans broke down the door late in the evening, accusing Yona of hiding some Jews. He denied it, of course. That day they had arrested a couple whose daughter, Paula Klein, was a staff member at the home but slept at home with her parents.

That evening, she had stayed late in the Tiefenbrunner Home, and the Germans, unaware that she was a legitimate employee with Gestapo-issued working papers, assumed that Yona was hiding her illegally. They took Paula to the Gestapo headquarters, where she was badly beaten, trying to pry out of her the address of her sister, who was living clandestinely. Finally the Gestapo phoned Yona to come and take her back.* The next day she returned to the Avenue Louise, the location of the Gestapo headquarters, in the effort to liberate her parents, but they had already been transferred to Malines and deported to their deaths.

Kurt Dressler, one of the older boys who served as Yona's personal secretary, recalls the Germans' frequent visits.** In early 1944, he was already considered overage and was ever fearful of being discovered. Kurt had personally witnessed the depths of Nazi savagery while out on one of his frequent errands for Monsieur and would take no chances with the Germans. He had seen it from afar, but the horrifying scene was indelibly carved into his memory.

The arrogant young German guard, nose upturned, rifle pointed, hollering "*Raus!*" (Out!) The young Jewish woman standing in the doorway of her home clutching an infant to her bosom, plaintively pleading, "Please! Let me just go back to get some clothing for my baby! It's cold outside!" In response, the beastly German cruelly yanks the wailing baby by its legs from the mother's arms and repeatedly beats the baby's head against the building's brick wall. Then, casually tossing the dead baby on the ground like a slaughtered chicken, he barks, "That's how we Germans take care of your babies. Now follow me or I'll shoot you here!"

* Paula Cappell-Klein survived and today is living in New York.

** This account was excerpted from a video testimonial by Kurt Dressler from the Yad Vashem archives.

Another time, Kurt was on the streetcar returning from an errand when he spotted the dreaded Gestapo cars and trucks up ahead, parked in front of the home. Instinctively, he jumped off the streetcar and took off running several blocks away, where he hid with sympathetic gentile neighbors. He remained there until evening, when he ascertained the coast was clear.

Kurt felt that his luck had run out. He asked Yona for help in finding him another place of refuge. Eventually Kurt joined the underground movement, where he participated in several daring attacks against the occupying Germans.*

* After the liberation, Kurt was reunited with his parents in America. They had escaped from Germany in 1939, shortly after sending Kurt on the *Kindertransport* to Belgium. They headed for Shanghai, the only place in the world at that time that allowed entry with neither a visa nor a passport. Along with 20,000 other Jewish refugees, including the Mirrer Yeshivah students, they had spent the war years in the Shanghai ghetto. After the war, they emigrated to America, and through the help of the Belgian Jewish Committee, they joyfully located their son. The family headed to America, where they rebuilt their lives. Kurt made his home in Toronto, Canada.

7
Liberation: Not a Moment Too Soon

The Nazis never abandoned their intention to deport the Jewish children. Despite the advancing Allied forces and the need to transport large numbers of troops via truck and train to fight their losing battle, their perverted drive to kill every last Jew compelled them to divert these precious resources to transport Jews to the concentration camps. In August of 1944, even as Allied troops were already nearing Belgium, SS Lieutenant Anton Burger, who had been sent to Belgium from Greece to deal with "Jewish matters," decided that all the registered Jews remaining in Belgium would have to be deported to concentration camps in the East.

The dreaded day had come: the German occupational government now reversed their policy of protecting the children in the AJB homes. Yona was fortunate to be tipped off by the AJB about the impending roundup of the children.*

It was a long night for Yona and Seligman Bamberger, as they worked feverishly into the wee hours of the morning, packing travel bags for

---

* Sylvain Brachfeld, "The Last Escape," from *Belgium and the Holocaust*, 428.

each child. The next day, a Sunday morning, the children left two by two so as not to attract attention. Yona told them that they were going to be hidden in a convent for a short while.

The convent was run by Father Robinet, a Catholic priest who was an acquaintance of Yona. The children were settled in the parochial hall, its benches removed and replaced with beds. The high, deep windows draped with heavy curtains provided privacy for the children to dress. Plates, dishes, and kosher food were brought over from the home. Mr. Bamberger also brought several pairs of tefillin and siddurim and *Chumashim* into the convent, which the older boys shared. Then the Tiefenbrunners, the Bambergers, and the rest of the staff dispersed, seeking individual hiding places in private homes.

Now the children were on their own. Being surrounded by statues and other Catholic religious icons was disconcerting, not to mention the rising fear that efforts might be made to force them to convert. And yet the children, taught by Yona to be staunch in their heritage, forged on. The first morning, immediately upon awakening, they got to their first order of business: davening *shacharis*.

Could they daven here? they requested of the priest. Permission was granted, but on the condition that they not conduct communal prayers, which might attract unwanted attention. Thus the children davened individually behind the thick curtains of the hall.

When Shabbos came, the older boys approached Father Robinet with a request. Could he find them a room where all the children could congregate for Shabbos davening? The priest gave them the use of his own office. It was on the third floor, so that in the event of the Germans arriving, there would be time to warn the children.

There, in the most unlikely of places — a priest's office in a building that had not ever before harbored holiness in the hundreds of years that it had stood, nor since — the boys conducted a heartwarming *Kabbalas Shabbos*, followed by a full Shabbos davening the next morning, complete with *leining* (from a *Chumash*).

The children found out later, at the farewell party following liberation, that Father Robinet had received instructions to convert them. But upon seeing that even without the presence of mentors these children continued to act as they had been taught — praying, keeping Shabbos, eating only kosher — he decided not to interfere. Till today, Father Robinet is remembered by those who stayed there for his kindness and integrity.

Two weeks later, on September 4, 1944, Brussels was liberated.

At first the Belgian population, who had witnessed many tanks and military vehicles driving on their roads over the last four years, did not take any notice when a new column of tanks began rolling through Brussels. They certainly did not expect the Allies to be anywhere near their city.

Upon closer examination, they noticed that the tanks looked different. They were British! The wonderful news spread like wildfire. The war was over! People from every house and building poured into the streets to welcome their liberators with hot food, fresh fruit, champagne, and flowers. The children, too, joined in the celebration. Monsieur was coming for them! No more worries! No more fears! Merrily singing and clapping, they marched back home to their beloved home at 34 Rue des Patriotes.

The streets of Brussels pulsated with the heady air of sheer joy during the immediate aftermath of the liberation. It was a time of reunions, of beginnings, of picking up the shattered pieces of their lives. Kurt Dressler was witness to an amazing family reunion in those days following liberation.

Belgian stamps issued on the occasion of victory, 1945

The Allies had asked Kurt, as a member of the underground resistance, to direct the heavy flow of traffic choking a main thoroughfare swarming with a motley blend of German and Allied vehicles and crowds of pedestrians — survivors — returning on foot from hiding. A little orphan child, probably from one of the children's homes in the area, approached Kurt, asking him whether he could help. It looked like great fun! Graciously, Kurt took the hand of the child, who waved the traffic flag enthusiastically, relishing the task.

An American jeep had stopped at their intersection. "Ask the soldier where he's from," the little boy begged Kurt. "My uncle lives in America. Maybe he knows him!"

As if this one American soldier would know the child's uncle in that vast country! But Kurt decided to humor him.

"From Brooklyn," answered the soldier kindly.

"My uncle lives in Brooklyn!" gushed the child, hopping with exuberant curiosity. "Maybe you know him? His name is David Rothstein!"*

Lieutenant Rothstein's eyes unleashed a torrent of joyful tears as he encircled his little nephew with a great hug. "I'm David, and you are the one I have been looking for!" Thus, one orphan child was reunited with his family in America.

As things settled down in the home, so did the gruesome realization gradually dawn that although the war was over, the liberation could never bring back their parents and family members. Among the six million victims were parents and families, forever gone with no parting words.

Close as the children were with one another — for many, these friendships lasted a lifetime — they seldom discussed the details of their families and the feelings of grief over the losses they had suffered. A protective shield of denial enabled them to maintain their sanity in the face of the enormity of their personal tragedies.**

Thus, though they knew there was no going backward to happier times, there was no obvious grieving. All they talked about was establishing new lives for themselves. Most intended to make aliyah to Israel, then British Palestine. They busied themselves with preparing to live in agricultural settlements in Israel. A good number of children did end up going to Israel, settling in the religious settlements of Kibbutz Chafetz

---

* Not his real name.

** It was only years later, long after the war, that those who had lived together in the Tiefenbrunner Home realized how little they had known of each other's backgrounds and families.

Chaim and Komemiyus, many of whom went on to raise beautiful generations of religious families.

Others were sent to America for adoption or to join relatives. In the cases where children were adopted, Yona ensured that they were fine, upstanding Jewish homes.

Children of the home who left for Israel, at the time still Palestine, August 1945. From right to left: Joseph Amsel, his brother Samuel, Rachel Kirschbaum, her brother Nathan, Helga Somer, her brother Manfred, Yona Tiefenbrunner, and Gaby Lehrer. Both Kirschbaums, both Somers, and Gaby Lehrer still live in Israel; they are married and have children and grandchildren, all of them shomrei Torah u'mitzvos.

Jules Rothschild remembers his parting with Yona after the liberation. "In March 1944, only months before the liberation, the Germans had grabbed my mother and sister, and I ended up at the home on Rue des Patriotes. I was brokenhearted, but Yona's presence comforted me. Thank G-d, my mother and sister survived and contacted me soon after the liberation.

"Yona accompanied me to the train station to see me off. I was only eleven years old. I was overcome with feelings of gratitude, but was at a loss as to how to express it. So I simply took his hand and kissed it, and I know he understood what my heart longed to convey."

8
Who Is That British Soldier?

One Friday afternoon, soon after the liberation, Yona made an announcement: a very special surprise guest would be joining them for Shabbos. He introduced a young smiling British soldier.

Who was this stranger? the children speculated. What was he doing here?

"This is my older brother, children. This is my long-lost brother Maurice whom I haven't seen in six years, since we left our home in Wiesbaden, Germany. *Baruch Hashem,* he survived the war!"

Maurice introduced himself, telling the spellbound children that he was indeed Yona's brother. Intrigued, they plied him with one question after another. How had he escaped Germany? Was he really a British soldier? How had he found Yona? Maurice promised the children that he would tell them the story of his entire ordeal after the meal.

The night was a memorable one. The children stayed up till the small hours of the morning, listening openmouthed as Maurice recounted his incredible story of *hashgachah pratis*, which, despite his travails, had enabled him to survive.

After our family's deportation to Poland from our home in Wiesbaden, I was left a homeless refugee, with no work and no friends. I decided to go to Belgium. There, both relatives and better financial opportunities awaited me. I sent my passport to my brother Phillip, who had contacts in the Belgian Embassy in Holland, for help in receiving a Belgian visa.

For days, I waited for my documents to be returned. To my relief, at long last, the package came from Phillip — but something marred my joy. My returned passport with the visa was due to expire the next day. How could I possibly arrive in Belgium within twenty-four hours, before my passport would be invalid? The only possibility was to take a train to Prague, where I would board a flight to Amsterdam and then take a short train ride from there to Antwerp.

Upon arriving in Prague with only minutes to spare, I frantically tried to obtain a seat on the overbooked KLM flight from Prague to Amsterdam, to no avail. Suddenly Eliyahu HaNavi came to my rescue in the form of an old man who offered me his seat, saying that due to a sudden emergency he would have to postpone his flight.

In Antwerp, I made my way on foot to Phillip's house, arriving in the early morning hours. As I approached the door, I overheard Yona and Phillip discussing my chances of making it in to Belgium. They knew my passport had expired the day before. Unable to contain myself, I burst in.

"Here I am!" I cried. That was all I managed to say before we fell into each other's arms.

Soon after, I became an apprentice diamond cutter. But in April 1939, I was caught by the Belgian police and faced with arrest and possible deportation for working as an illegal alien without a permit. All too soon, I found myself on the run again.

I managed to contact Jewish agents of the Irgun, the underground Jewish defense force that would later become part of the Israeli army, and joined an illegal transport of Jewish refugees to British Palestine.

Via Paris and Marseilles, I made it onto a ship with a group of twenty others, eventually setting sail on the SS *Parita*, a converted cargo ship.

The scheduled ten-day trip turned into a veritable nightmare as the smugglers, ever hungry for financial profits, accepted an additional seven hundred and fifty passengers on a ship meant for two hundred and fifty. To make matters worse, we were informed that the boat would not take us to our intended destination, but would meet up with several small sailing boats in Cyprus, which would transfer us to the port of Haifa. (The crew hoped to turn back to Europe and make some additional illegal trips.)

For days, we waited at the designated meeting place near Cyprus, but no boats arrived. The food supply ran out. Conditions aboard the miserably overcrowded ship deteriorated rapidly. Many of the elderly and children fell dangerously ill from malnutrition and unsanitary conditions.

After seventy days of wandering (instead of the intended ten), shuttling back and forth between several Middle Eastern ports and begging for food from passing ocean liners (including twenty bottles of beer from one passing cruise ship), our group commandeered a ship from a Greek crew, hoisted the blue-and-white Magen David flag, and beached the vessel on the shores of Tel Aviv in late August 1939. It was a Friday night, and thousands of people came out to greet us with food.

I was penniless and physically weak, but in buoyant spirits upon reaching the shores of the Holy Land. My joy was short-lived when the British coast guards came running, attempting to push the boat back into the sea. But their attempts failed; before landing, the group on board, anticipating the intervention of the British, had smashed all the engines with sledgehammers to prevent just that.

All the passengers were interned by the British in a military camp. We had been in the camp for just ten days when, on September 3, 1939, Britain declared war against Germany. Amnesty was declared, and I was free at last and a legal Palestinian citizen.

I soon got a job, but my thoughts centered on my family, whom I had left behind to an unknown fate. News of the plight of Polish Jewry was beginning to filter through. I wanted desperately to do something personally to help. But what could I do from thousands of miles away?

When I heard from friends that the British army was accepting new recruits, I felt that here was my answer: I would join a fighting force and do my personal share of eradicating Nazi evil.

This was the start of a new adventure for me. I, along with many of my comrades, joined the Pioneer Corps. In 1940, I was part of the historic Dunkirk Evacuation in Dunkirk, France, in which over 330,000 British troops were evacuated back to England. Regrouped at the military camp in Aldershot (a small town about thirty-five miles from London), I joined the 51st Middle East commando, which was dispatched to Africa to fight the Axis powers, Germany and Italy. As a British soldier, I fought in the Ethiopian cities of Gondar, Kerendnar, and Kern.

Soon I was promoted to corporal. Injured while trying to rescue a wounded comrade, I was transferred to a nearby hospital to recover. Two weeks later I rejoined my unit, whose task was to patrol the area, on the lookout for Italian pockets of resistance. During one of our patrols, we came upon a village with a large clan of Ethiopian Jews. These people were living in abject poverty under the most primitive conditions. Some of the soldiers who spoke Arabic managed to converse with the villagers. Hearing that the soldiers had come from Palestine, they assumed that we were Mashiach's soldiers coming to liberate them!

Maurice Tiefenbrunner in his uniform of the 51st Commando, 1941

Finally my unit left Africa, arriving in Egypt. In December 1941, I participated in an early raid on Tobruk, Libya, where we inflicted heavy Italian casualties before withdrawing. Now down to one-third of its strength, my unit was disbanded in Geneifa, Egypt.

It was then that I was recruited by British Intelligence officer Captain Bruck to join the newly formed SIG — the Special Interrogation Group made up of German-speaking volunteers from Palestine. Our mission was to don German uniforms and go undercover to perform special acts of sabotage.

This was the opportunity I had been waiting for, to play a direct role in fighting the Germans. That was my reason for joining the British army!

I did participate in numerous raids that succeeded in killing many Germans — until I was taken prisoner in December 1942 and spent the next two and a half years in captivity as a POW in Italy.

Although I was joined by several other Jewish soldiers, there was no Jewish life in the POW camp. There was no possibility of keeping Shabbos, kashrus, or *yamim tovim*. Still, I made every effort to fulfill the mitzvos as best as I could under those trying conditions. On Shabbos, I and my Jewish comrades would try to do the least work possible without being caught. And everyone knew me as the one who liked to exchange his meat tins (filled with pork or bacon) for sardines.

Thanks to the rules of the Geneva Convention, which established universal standards for the treatment of POWs, conditions were harsh but not life-threatening. There was a constant battle with the mice and rats in the decrepit barracks. The rodents would get into any scrap food left out, so we resorted to hanging up washing lines and clipping our food parcels on them. The rats were unable to balance on the thin lines, but mice had no trouble. It was a common sight to behold — the mice climbing up and gnawing their way through the rope until the food packages fell to the floor, where they rushed for it. They were everywhere, unavoidable. One morning I was putting my shoes on and stepped onto a mouse hiding inside my shoe!

In September 1943, as the fighting in Italy turned in favor of the Allies, there was talk among the senior officers of the camp. Soon the news spread like wildfire: they would abandon camp, march south, and surrender to the Americans.

I could already taste the sweet flavor of freedom, but alas! My high hopes were dashed when at five a.m., on the morning that we were scheduled to commence our march, in trooped the Germans, taking over the camp. They had been tipped off about the impending surrender, and they had come to transfer the prisoners to a location under German control.

With the usual German efficiency, the evacuation was organized within hours. The prisoners were packed onto a freight train, fifty men per boxcar, and transported across the border into Austria, which was, of course, fully occupied by German troops. Some of us tried to climb out of the little windows in the wagon in an effort to escape, but we were recaptured the moment we jumped to the ground.

After enduring two miserable days in unbearable conditions on the train, we arrived at a POW camp in southern Austria. But with the Russians advancing on the eastern front and Americans on the western front, we were constantly on the move. Time and again we were transferred further and further into Germany.

During the autumn of 1944, we began what was to be our final march. Under heavy guard, we marched for three weeks with barely any food or drink and no protection from the elements. Many prisoners collapsed by the wayside, never to rise again.

Our destination was Fallingbostle, an army camp in close proximity to Hanover. Within a few days, we were joined by more POWs who had been evacuated from Stalag 7, another German POW camp that had held many American airmen, as well as British, Canadian, Russian, and Polish POWs.

I was glad to meet soldiers from Palestine whom I knew from the early days of my army life. We immediately got to work on counterintelligence, as well as establishing radio contact with the British army. With some experts among us who fashioned a crude radio, we were soon able to hear BBC news and maintain daily contact with the First British Army, becoming fully acquainted with developments on the front. The radio transmitter was never discovered, despite the Germans breaking into our barracks numerous times, ripping open floors, searching with dogs, and threatening terrible punishment. They didn't find it because it was strategically buried under the hut of the German chief commanding officer!

With our constant source of news, at last the certainty was established that with the second front being opened, the war could not last much longer. It became manifest by the attitudes of the German guards. As their position grew increasingly hopeless, they became friendlier.

One day, during the month of February 1945, the Germans informed us of their worsening position. With the British army advancing toward the camp, the guards surrendered to the prisoners, agreeing to hand over all their weapons and ammunition. Tempting as it was, we refrained from breaking out of the camp for fear of roaming SS officers. But we didn't have much longer to wait. Only days later the British arrived, which spelled freedom at last.

I made my way back to Belgium to find my brothers. But how to locate the whereabouts of Yona and Phillip? I headed for the Jewish community center, a beehive of activity buzzing with conversation in a multitude of languages.

Apparently I wasn't the only one looking for family. There were soldiers of all nationalities, concentration camp survivors, and others who had come out of hiding. Hundreds of people swarmed around the information desk, looking for their parents, brothers, sisters, children, and other relatives. When my turn came, I was given a form to fill in the names and addresses of the persons I wished to find.

"Why are you looking for Yona Tiefenbrunner?" queried the clerk. She eyed me, sizing up the British soldier facing her.

When I told her that Yona was my brother, she fixed me with a strange look and asked me to wait. She had to make a phone call, she said. How perplexing! Why couldn't she simply complete the form for me as everyone else had done?

The woman did not return, but within five minutes, there came Yona! Overwhelmed, we fell into each other's arms.

As it turned out, Yona was one of the leading people of the committee, and at the moment I had come looking for my family, Yona had been working in a different room in the same building!

With this, the special guest dressed in a British army uniform concluded his tale. The children were heartened to know that one of their own had succeeded in killing the enemy who had caused them so much suffering during the long years of war.

Peering into their hungry eyes, Maurice spent hours with them. Time and sleep were forgotten as he patiently answered their endless questions until the wee hours of the morning. He spent most of his stay in Belgium bonding with the children, who benefited greatly from his charisma and warmth, until he left for London to sign off on his army duties.

Maurice with the children

9
A New Chapter

In May 1945, a new crisis arose in Belgium: dealing with two thousand orphaned Jewish children. Following the war, a flood of impoverished and brokenhearted survivors of the camps, children among them, were streaming into Belgium. In addition, orphaned children who had been hidden in private Catholic homes, institutions, and monasteries in Belgium during the war were located and handed over to the Brussels Jewish community.* Many of these homeless children were directed to the Tiefenbrunners.

Ever the faithful shepherd, Yona knew that these children had special needs both emotionally and spiritually. Even though, at the close of the war, Yona — then thirty-one years old and in the prime of his life — could have decided he'd done enough as a public servant, he recommitted himself to the *klal.*

Thus began a new chapter in the life of the father of orphans. He founded a new children's home in Mariaburg, a suburb of Antwerp. It

* Countless Jewish children hidden in Christian institutions, including orphanages and monasteries, were forever lost to the Jewish people. Their parents and close relatives had all perished in the Holocaust. When rabbis or distant relatives finally tracked down many of these children, the priests and nuns who had been their caretakers insisted that there were no Jewish children with them.

was established with the central Belgian Jewish Committee under the auspices of Agudath Israel and the Poalei Agudas Yisroel movement.

Yona with two of "his" children outside the Mariaburg home

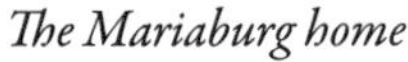

The Mariaburg home

Yona was undaunted by the herculean task of rehabilitating the "*lebedige korbanos*," the living victims of the war. Life was difficult enough for an orphan — who lacked the soul-fortifying, individualized care that only parents can give — to grow into a healthy young adult. But that paled in comparison to the cataclysmic traumas many of Yona's new charges had suffered in early childhood. They'd witnessed the brutal murders of their parents and loved ones. They'd been subjected to living in squalor, suffering starvation, and enduring the stark fear of the ghettos, where young and old expired daily from hunger.

Those who had survived the camps, in addition to witnessing their own suffering, had seen adults — completely stripped of their human dignity and subjected to enslavement, torture, disease, starvation, and murder — break down and snap. They had seen the adults in power — police, informers, soldiers — act barbarically to others instead of protecting them. Some had been hidden with lawless partisans in the forests, living not unlike animals, subsisting on grass and wild vegetation.

It was little wonder that many of the children were deeply troubled, even psychologically scarred. They viewed adults with hostility and suspicion, refusing to receive help or guidance from them, which gave rise to discipline problems. Many exhibited unethical behaviors — such as lying, stealing, and smuggling — that had become absolutely critical for survival during wartime, but now needed to be uprooted. One boy, eleven years old, was brought to Yona's home following a rash of killings he had just committed. A survivor of Bergen-Belsen, he was so filled with rage that after liberation, he had managed to obtain a gun and murder some Germans!

In addition, the children who had been reclaimed from Catholic caregivers were in grave danger of being lost to *Yiddishkeit*. The Christian monasteries and orphanages had made a concerted effort to convert the Jewish children who had been given to them for safekeeping. Many of the children were even being trained to become members of the Catholic clergy. During the war, they had been told that their lives hinged on concealing their Jewish origins, and their only hope, in the event of another outbreak of murderous fury directed at the Jews, lay in living as devout Catholics.

Even the children in private homes had been markedly influenced by the practices of their gentile caregivers. Many of these children came to the Tiefenbrunner Home refusing at first to abandon their Christian rituals and relinquish the crosses they wore.

Some of the boys who came to the home after the war had not had a bris. At the onset of the war, parents giving birth to sons did not have their babies circumcised in the effort to hide their Jewishness. Yona took upon himself to give these boys a bris and enter them into the covenant of Avraham Avinu.

Chana Kaufman and her friend Irena were rescued from a convent by Irena's grandfather. He searched for a suitable Jewish home for the girls, a religious institution that would educate them in Torah and mitzvos while providing them with a warm, homey atmosphere to replace the family lives they had lost. The Brussels Jewish committee recommended an orphanage that met Irena's grandfather's requirements. He was very satisfied, but Chana was apprehensive — again a new place! She was fifteen years old in 1945 and, having been through so much, was wary of starting all over again.

Yona welcomed them warmly. "Welcome, dear girls! We're very happy that you came to join all our children," he said in the friendliest way. That was the start of the wonderful years Chana spent in the orphanage, at such a critical time in her life, where she reconnected with *Yiddishkeit.**

Jacquelyn Cox also came to the home after being rescued from a convent. Her story was tragic. She was born in a Brussels hospital in 1942. The bestial Nazis were performing a hospital raid just then, looking for Jews. They deported her mother — who had just given birth — to Auschwitz, placing newborn Jacquelyn in a convent. After the war, Yona collected her from the convent. It turned out that Jacqueline had siblings who were hidden by Christians and had come together to the *Kinderheim* after the war. But they never bonded with their younger sister, since they hadn't grown up with her. Life dealt harshly with Jacqueline: when she grew up, her siblings lost contact with her, and she remained childless after marrying in London. But Jacquelyn, who was often lonely, was always smiling, always answering, "*Baruch Hashem*," always ready to help others. Faigy Hochhauser (Reitzer), who lives in London, would invite her often.

"The only family she ever referred to was Mr. Tiefenbrunner," says Faigy. "Just as people quote their father's *minhagim* at a Seder table, she would invariably say, 'Monsieur did it this way...Monsieur did it that way.' "**

Many children had lost out on years of schooling, which compounded the problem of reintegrating them into a normal social framework and classroom settings.

---

* Recounted from Chana (Kaufman) Zucker's book, *Behind the Walls.*

** Jacqueline passed away a few years ago. It was thanks to Yona Tiefenbrunner that she lived and was buried as a Jew. An amazing story is told about Jacqueline after her death, heard firsthand from her sister-in-law. A short time after Jacqueline died, her sister-in-law dreamed of her. Jacqueline told her that she had borrowed a book from the library and hadn't given it back. She told her where the book was and asked her sister-in-law to return it to the library since she was not allowed to enter Gan Eden unless the book was returned. Her sister-in-law didn't pay attention to the dream at first, but the dream repeated itself a few days later. She went to Jacqueline's apartment, found the book, and returned it to the library, and the dreams stopped. How amazing that a person who was considered a "simple" Jew here on earth was given the opportunity to correct a deed that seems inconsequential to us, in order to allow her to access Gan Eden!

Kalman Jung and his sister spent the war in the nonreligious Wezembeek children's home. They were two of the fifty-eight children who were delivered to the infamous Malines camp in October 1942. The night they arrived, they were scheduled to join the sixteenth convoy to Auschwitz, but were saved by the prompt intervention of Queen Elizabeth and sent to the children's home. After the war, their older brother, who had escaped to Switzerland during the war, located Kalman and his sister with the help of the Red Cross, and they were placed in the Mariaburg home of Yona Tiefenbrunner.

Kalman knew nothing of *Yiddishkeit* when he arrived in Mariaburg at the age of nine. He had been separated from his parents since he was four years old and had been living in the nonreligious environment of Wezembeek ever since. Who would think that he would become a *yeshivah bachur*?

Yona Tiefenbrunner did. He worried over Kalman like he would his own child, seeing to his every need. Kalman lived with Yona for six years, until he left for the *yeshivah gedolah* in Koepeln at the age of fifteen.*

Alfred Friedman and his two sisters also came to the home after the war, and it is due to Yona that they reclaimed their Jewish heritage. After their father was nabbed by the Germans in Brussels, their mother placed them in a Belgian convent for the duration of the war for safekeeping. When their mother failed to show up after Brussels's liberation, it was presumed that she had been one of the victims in Auschwitz. A distant cousin who had returned from hiding located the Friedman children and placed them in the Tiefenbrunner Home in Mariaburg. That's where Alfred and his sister were reacquainted with everything Jewish.**

---

* Today Kalman Jung lives in Bnei Brak. He has a large *chassidishe* family of eight children and many grandchildren and great-grandchildren.

** Alfred's story is tinged with a different kind of tragedy. In 1947, Alfred, then a teenager, and his younger sister were sent to a family in the U.S. Through all the years of growing up parentless, they always believed that their mother had perished in the war. Then, in 2005, Alfred's son, Sholom, on a trip to Auschwitz, made a startling discovery. Upon reviewing the Nazi records, he learned that his grandmother had indeed survived and had been repatriated to Belgium after the war. Further research led them to municipal records in Brussels and a letter dated December 12, 1946, allowing their mother permission to enter Belgium to search for her lost children. But, alas, she was never accounted for again. Alfred has made numerous efforts, checking

Today Alfred's son, Rabbi Shalom Friedman, is the director of the Torah Umesorah Holocaust Curriculum.*

Yes, it was Yona who responded to the call of the hour, taking in these wretched, homeless, tempest-tossed children. Against all odds, Yona persevered in ministering to them, his single objective to raise children who would continue on the ancient path of their martyred parents, to be the link to the next generation of Torah-true Jews.

Yona was a strategic organizer. He mobilized a team of teachers and educators around him who would assist him in his holy and difficult task of restoring these lost, broken *neshamos*. One by one, he selected only those imbued with a tremendous spirit of *Yiddishkeit* to work alongside him.

Lithuanian-born Reb Yissachar David, a *yerei Shamayim* and today one of the prominent members of the Jewish community of Antwerp, was a survivor of the camps who came to teach the boys Gemara during the first few summers after the war.

In those immediate postwar days, Chassidus was conspicuously absent in Belgium. The great chassidic courts of Europe had been decimated. The Rebbes who had escaped the Nazi cauldron had not yet managed to regroup and rebuild from the ashes of the *churban*. And yet, some of those who found their way to the *Kinderheim* after the war, individuals of various chassidic circles, managed to breathe the unique chassidic warmth and vivacity into the boys.

Reb Wolf Berkowicz, *z"l*, a Gerrer chassid living in Brussels, taught the boys *limudei kodesh* twice a week. Then there was Reb Akiva Yosef Stein, a Vizhnitzer chassid. And Reb Mendel Landau, today an esteemed Bobover chassid and an Auschwitz survivor, not only reviewed Gemara

all the hospital and old-age-home records in Belgium, to locate her or learn when and where she passed away, to no avail. Was she wantonly murdered by anti-Semitic hooligans in the anarchy of the war's aftermath? Was she living, ill and alone, somewhere — perhaps in a different country — all these years? The recent revelation that she had come close to being reunited with them and then disappeared and the open-ended question of whether she's still alive continues to torment Alfred.

* Alfred is living today in Oro Valley, Arizona.

with the boys, but also taught the boys some deeply inspiring Bobover *niggunim*.

Reb Mendel personified the fire of *deveikus* and the devotion to HaKadosh Baruch Hu that Chassidus had imbued him with — the Chassidus he had absorbed all through childhood and young adulthood at his Rebbe's *tisch*. This was the bedrock that had sustained his faith through his tribulations in Auschwitz. Now this passion, this love of Hashem, he imparted to the boys.

When he taught the boys the soul-stirring Bobover *niggunim*, including the legendary "*Shir HaMa'aalos Esa Einai*," the boys discovered the power of the *chassidishe niggun* to heal their tormented souls. And its effects were far-reaching: some of those boys would grow up to become patriarchs of prominent chassidic families.

The children and staff posing in front of their beloved Mariaburg home

10

Is It Possible to Sing?

Yona's family was growing — his younger two daughters, Judith and Mariette, were born in 1945 and 1947. Ruth had her hands full caring for their three little ones, and so Yona knew he needed to rely on supportive *madrichos* to help nurture and mentor the rest of the children emotionally and spiritually. Over the years, the staff of the *Kinderheim* included a number of noble and warm *madrichos,* who served as counselors and surrogate mothers. Miriam Zupnick, *a"h*, one of the first, stands out among them.

" '*Modeh ani lefanecha...*' The sun is shining, *kinderlach*. The war is over. There's no reason to fear anything anymore... Forget your nightmares. Wake up and sing with me to Hashem..."

The sweet angelic voice of Mademoiselle Miriam resounded each morning as she threaded her way through the bedrooms, tapping shoulders and stroking cheeks.

Miriam Censor, a Polish girl from a family of Belzer chassidim, was a survivor of Bergen-Belsen and Auschwitz. After liberation, she came to Belgium and became one of the first staff members of the new

Tiefenbrunner Home in Mariaburg. Blonde-haired, blue-eyed twenty-five-year-old Miriam was as kind, sensitive, and warmhearted as she was beautiful.

Even in the darkness of Bergen-Belsen, her character shone through like a brilliant ray of light. During roll call for the infamous *selektzias*, when, with a flick of a thumb, the inmates deemed unfit for labor were sent to the gas chambers, Miriam would prick her finger, drawing blood to rosy up the cheeks of her friends. She would physically lift them up so they stood straight and erect to avoid being singled out for death.

When a young woman in her barracks became deathly ill with typhoid, Miriam took care of her. At great peril, she stole potatoes from the kitchen, cooked them by placing them under the stove in the barracks, and fed them to the sick woman. Once, Miriam was caught by the *kapo*. Because she was such a good worker, the *kapo* told her she'd turn a blind eye this one time. But one more time, and she would be hanged! Possessed of an overpowering sense of *mesiras nefesh*, Miriam continued to procure the potatoes, and the young woman was nursed back to health, spared from certain death. Little wonder that she'd earned the reputation in Auschwitz as "the *Malach*" — the Angel!

With the progression of the Allied war efforts, the munitions plant where Miriam was working at the time was targeted for bombings. One of Miriam's coworkers, who was also her dearest friend, began crying bitterly. She bemoaned the fact that her child, who was hidden with gentiles, would never know that he had a Jewish mother, because the munitions plant would be the first to be bombed and they would all die before war's end. Miriam, who had somehow managed to hide her platinum ring, used it then to bribe an officer to have her friend reassigned. She could have used the ring to save herself, but she had no children yet and so selflessly sacrificed her sole bargaining chip to save her friend.

They both survived the war, and Miriam's dear friend was reunited with her child, who lived to raise children and grandchildren.

In the summer of 1945, Miriam found herself temporarily living in Brussels in a Red Cross apartment. It would have been natural for her to devote her time to nursing her own wounds. But this was not the stuff of which Miriam was fashioned. She was determined to express her appreciation to the Almighty for having spared her life by aiding those even less fortunate than herself.

Someone mentioned to Miriam that if she was seeking employment, a good opportunity was at hand: the newly established children's home for Holocaust survivors and orphans in the neighboring suburb of Mariaburg. She obtained the address and made her way there to meet with the director.

Yona, critically selective in hiring compassionate and skilled staff, quickly discerned Miriam's personality. Immediately grasping that she would be the perfect antidote for the children under his care, he welcomed her with open arms. Soon enough Yona was gratified to realize that he couldn't have found a better candidate for the job.

The next day, when Miriam came to the home, she found a disparate group of children. Grief-stricken, shattered camp survivors who seemed walled in by the terrifying memories of what they had witnessed in the death camps. Sulking, miserable children, who had been removed from the Catholic homes where they had been hidden as toddlers and — remembering neither their original parents, nor the fact that they were Jewish — grieving over being separated from their "parents." And then there were those brooding children — sometimes several siblings together — who had been dropped off at the home in the immediate aftermath of the war. Their single surviving parent possessed neither the financial means nor the emotional energy to care for his children during those difficult times.

No one smiled, let alone sang. They had lost all sense of childhood. To play? To sing? To express feelings of joy and exhilaration? They could not do it.

Yes, Miriam had her work cut out for her, but she wasn't daunted. She was the flame, the catalyst, that rekindled hope, rebirth, and renewal. It wasn't long before Miriam's inner joy and resilience of spirit seeped into the children. Miriam, too, had lost her entire family in the Nazi inferno, and yet she had overcome the horrors. If she could sing, so could they.

Indeed, with her kind and gentle nature, she had an uncanny ability in enabling the children to forget, or at least partially erase, their nightmarish experiences and overcome their deep and great sorrows.

Goldine was one of the unhappy little children who arrived in the home in early 1946, a little knapsack full of Belgian chocolates strung across her shoulders and a necklace with a cross on her neck. Goldine was nearly seven years old, and she was fretful and miserable at having to part from "Aunt Delphine."

Goldine Ehrenfeld was born in 1939 in Germany. Her parents were originally from Poland. After Kristallnacht, it became clear to all German Jews that they could no longer stay even one more day. Her parents arranged for a smuggler to get them into neighboring Belgium, but he refused to take the two youngest of their four children — six-month-old Goldine and her two-year-old brother.

How to get the little ones over the border? Goldine's aunt Betty, her mother's sister, who already had tickets to board a ship to America, devised a plan. She pinned name tags on the two babies and put them on a train to Belgium. It was a short ride — only an hour's distance — and Goldine's uncle, who had been living in Belgium since 1933, when he'd fled Germany, would be waiting at the Brussels station to take them off the train.

Baby Goldine and her toddler brother were thus reunited with their parents in Antwerp, and life became routine for the Ehrenfeld family. Even after May 1940, when the German occupation of Belgium began, things remained largely as they had been before, for a time. The lull after occupation deceived most Belgian Jews, and they could not see the handwriting on the wall. Goldine's aunt in America sent visas for the entire family, pleading with them to emigrate to America. But they could not come up with enough funds to purchase the fare for passage, and so they remained.

With the progression of the Nazis' decrees against the Jews, many began fleeing to France, among them Goldine's uncle and family. The Ehrenfelds made plans to escape to Switzerland.

But it was not meant to be. In August 1942, Goldine's father was arrested and deported for "compulsory labor in his country of origin." Goldine's mother was left alone with the four little children. There was no way she could flee on her own with her young charges, and so she had no recourse but to contemplate the worst-case scenario as she understood it.

An immigrant who comprehended little of the Flemish announcements that blared daily now in the streets, she believed the outrageous lie that families were being relocated in the east. They said that special communities would be established, in which the adults would work to support the war effort; their children would be sent to school while the parents would be working. Where would the Germans place Goldine? she wondered. Goldine wasn't quite four years old yet; she wasn't old enough to attend school.

Mrs. Ehrenfeld made a heartrending decision: there was no choice but to temporarily part with Goldine. Tearfully, and with a prayer in her heart, she approached her Belgian gentile housekeeper, Delphine. Delphine had worked devotedly for the extended family for many years and was considered extremely trustworthy. Would she take Goldine home with her and keep her safe until their return?

Goldine loved Delphine very much, had known her since her early childhood. She was very excited about going to spend some time with Delphine in the wide open fields and fresh air of the Antwerp suburb where Delphine and her husband lived.

Only days later, Goldine's mother and siblings were taken away and sent to Auschwitz. Goldine was never told. She spent her days frolicking in the garden and playing with friends.

When Delphine went to church, Goldine joined her and grew to enjoy the weekly trip. She was vaguely aware that something was atypical about her, because Delphine didn't allow her to do communion. "You're different" was the simple answer Goldine received from Delphine when she asked why not. It didn't dawn on Goldine what "different" meant.

As the war progressed in 1944, Antwerp faced severe food shortages. Delphine found it hard to adequately nourish Goldine, a growing child. Then she heard rumors that the AJB was handing out ration cards for Jewish children.

Delphine made her way to the AJB offices and duly registered her name and the Jewish child's name on whose behalf she had requested the ration cards. Blissfully, she left with the free ration cards for milk, eggs, and cheese stowed in her purse.

She never dreamed that she was feeding right into the Germans' trap! Soon the Gestapo, armed with the AJB list and her telltale signature verifying her address, came marching to Delphine's house in search of their quarry: innocent Goldine.

Somehow Delphine succeeded in hiding Goldine. Although the Nazis didn't find her, they imprisoned Delphine in a Belgian jail for collaboration with the underground and sheltering a Jewish child. It was only due to the efforts of Delphine's husband, who bribed the local Belgian prison guard, that Delphine wasn't deported to Malines and subsequently to Auschwitz.

Goldine was sent to Delphine's sister-in-law in Bruges, an oceanside town. Then, one day, the family was taking a tram ride when a few German soldiers boarded.

"Looks like a Jewish child," they remarked. That was all it took for Delphine's sister-in-law to get off at the next stop with Goldine. She would take no more chances sheltering a Jewish girl, and she placed Goldine in a convent school.

Shortly afterward came liberation. Delphine was freed from prison and dutifully went in search of Goldine. Soon they were joyfully reunited. Goldine returned to Delphine's home, where she was lovingly cared for. For her birthday, Delphine bought her a lovely necklace — a cross.

One day Goldine's uncle, Chaim Zev Feldman, knocked on the door. Delphine welcomed him warmly, and over coffee and cookies served on her best china, she related how Goldine had been kept out of German reach.

Delphine would have dearly liked to keep "Goldintje," then a beautiful six-year-old girl with cascading dark curls. But Goldine's stay at the convent had left its mark, and during that first visit already, it was clear that she had been indoctrinated. Mr. Feldman convinced Delphine that Goldine belonged with her people and should be moved to a Jewish home.

The problem was that Goldine's uncle was hardly in a position to take in Goldine. He had been widowed from his wife and daughters and had just returned, penniless and shattered, with his teenage son and was struggling to rebuild his life.

They pondered the situation for a bit, and they decided to place Goldine in the Tiefenbrunner Home until Mr. Feldman would be able to adopt her. Goldine's aunt Betty in America raised money to redeem her little niece so she might grow up Jewish. With the money Betty sent, they reimbursed Delphine for the expenses accrued in keeping Goldine.

Soon after, six-year-old Goldine, youthfully innocent and very unhappy about leaving, was brought to the Tiefenbrunner Home.

How miserable Goldine felt, to be abandoned in a strange orphanage! What's more, she was totally unfamiliar with the Jewish environment. She felt Christian and had no clue as to what Jewish was. How she missed her Aunt Delphine, her mother figure for the last three years! She was here alone, without siblings from whom to draw comfort. How she longed to go back home to her Aunt Delphine!

It was Miriam who came to the rescue, stepping in as a surrogate mother. She lavished the sulking little girl with affectionate hugs, boundless patience, and genuine love. Slowly Goldine learned about Hashem and davening the Jewish way with *berachos*, "*Modeh Ani*," and Shema, though she continued to wear her necklace with the cross, her connection with the only past she remembered.

Miriam never pressured her to remove it. She recognized the voluminous tumult of emotions in Goldine's little heart and knew the only antidote was more love and more patience. Her efforts were rewarded. The day arrived when Goldie voluntarily took it off, saying she no longer needed it.

Some months later, Goldine's uncle remarried and adopted her. She continued studying in the Yesodei Hatorah school until her marriage, when she moved to New York. Today Goldine is a true mother of Israel, whose children and grandchildren are prominent members of the yeshivah world.

Eight-year-old Brunia Singer came to the home in 1945, another post–World War II arrival.

Five years earlier, in 1940, four-year-old Brunia, her parents, and her newborn brother, Yankel, escaped their native Krakow. In 1942, Brunia's mother was deported and perished in the Belzec death camp. Her brokenhearted father, a Belzer chassid, received a *berachah* from the Belzer Rebbe that he and his two little children would survive.

Indeed, it was a long, twisted path of outright miracles that assured their survival against high odds. They survived two ghettos — the Krakow and Bochnia ghettos. And they survived Bergen-Belsen.

Because Brunia's father had heard that the Nazis respected foreign citizens, he somehow managed to procure Argentinean papers.* As "stateless" citizens, they were interned in a special section of Bergen-Belsen reserved for prisoners of war.**

As was the case with all children who were suddenly confronted with the cataclysmic upheaval of the shocking wartime tragedies, Brunia had grown emotionally mature overnight. Immediately she intuited her father's grief, compounded by the worry over who would now care for his two young orphaned children. She understood in her little heart that under the duress of the inhumane conditions in the camp, her father was completely demoralized.

And so, at the age of six, she vowed to herself not to exhibit emotional neediness to her father so as not to burden him unnecessarily. Moreover, she deemed herself responsible for mothering her two-year-old brother, Yankel.

How she and her toddler brother — two starving creatures with huge, frightened eyes — survived for two years in the camps, while her father and all the other men were marched out to forced labor, is an altogether miraculous story.

For two and a half years, these two little children endured without any of the rudiments of child care — lacking nutrition, sanitary conditions, immunizations, heat in the cold winters, clothing, not to mention emotional tending. They would be left alone all day in the barracks, barely uttering a sound to avoid unwanted attention.

In early April 1945, when the Allied armies advanced beyond the

* The Nazis seemed willing to accept that foreign citizens, even Jews — citizens of Western countries across the Atlantic and the neutral counties of Sweden and Switzerland — could be exempt from anti-Jewish edicts.

** Among the other inmates in this camp were the Bluzhever Rebbe and Rebbetzin Esther Jungreis and her parents.

Rhine River and began slicing into central Germany, the guards at Bergen-Belsen panicked. They hurriedly crammed 2,500 political prisoners — the Singers among them — into boxcars of an old freight train, as many as sixty-eight to a car. Their torturous journey was to take them still deeper into Germany, beyond the Elbe River (where the Allies hadn't reached yet). Their destination: another death camp where they could be eliminated.

Again *Hashgachah* intervened. On April 13, 1945, after nearly a week on board, the German trainmen got into an argument over the route, and the cars were shunted onto the siding deep in the forest, a few miles near the town of Magdeburg. It was there, on that same day, that a small task force of two light tanks of the American 743rd Tank Battalion, led by Major Clarence Benjamin on a routine patrolling mission, came upon hundreds of shabby-looking civilians — families with children — by the side of the road. Upon seeing the American tank, the larger force of SS troopers fled.*

In bits and pieces, amid an outpouring of laughter and emotions of pure relief, the newly freed prisoners told their story. Many of them, though dressed in civilian clothing, were starving, emaciated creatures. They had been on the train for nearly a week with virtually no nourishment. A few had tragically perished on board. The Americans ordered the German farmers of the surrounding towns to stay up all night if necessary to get food for the people. They also appropriated the local homes for the survivors' temporary use.

Brunia recalls the childish sensation of glee she felt when she lay on a proper bed after sleeping on hardwood planks in Bergen-Belsen for two and a half years. "It was like sinking into a cloud!"

Where to pick up the torn threads of life? Survivors drifted to nearby Belgium — the war had been over there for over a year, and Jewish communal life had already been rehabilitated. Brunia's father heard about the Tiefenbrunner Home, and he hurried to bring them there so he could focus on rebuilding his shattered life.

Brunia, then eight, and her brother Yankel, four, were the fourth and fifth children to arrive in the post–World War II Tiefenbrunner Home

* Excerpted from Wayne Robinson's *Move Out, Verify,* 162–63, from the Hudson Falls World War II Living History Project.

in 1945. Since Brunia had taken her mother's place in caring for Yankel from the time they'd lost their mother when he was but two, he had grown accustomed to relying on her for his every need. Now, upon arriving in a strange new place, he clung to her relentlessly, terrified of facing a new life without the comforting presence of his sister.

Site of the train liberated by the 743rd Tank Battalion. The boxcars that had been derailed can be seen.

Mademoiselle Miriam understood that it was imperative to separate these "Siamese twins." This was no easy endeavor, but Miriam devised a variety of different methods to draw Yankel's attention away from his sister. Gently and consistently, Miriam employed her charm and wisdom to wean Yankel from his Brunia. To win this campaign, she amassed an arsenal of toys, treats, and goodies, and she used them generously.

Brunia remembers feeling a tremendous sense of *Yiddishkeit* permeating the home when she arrived — a sensation that left her exulted with the feeling of belonging, of coming home. All along she had known that she was a Jewish child, but the war had robbed her both of the early years of schooling and the possibilities of performing the mitzvos and celebrating *yamim tovim*. How beautiful, how new, were those

Left: A group of the freed prisoners in front of the boxcar train. Right: people running to greet their liberators the moment they realized they were free. (Photos taken by Major Clarence Benjamin at the scene and reprinted here courtesy of the Hudson Falls High School World War II Living History project)

first traces of genuine *Yiddishkeit* that were unfolding in front of her day by day!

Brunia now longed to use her gifted intelligence to learn. Thus far, her brainpower had been channeled exclusively toward survival, toward caring for her brother. She entered a classroom for the first time at the age of eight. So eager was she to swallow the learning that every day Brunia would burst into tears at the teacher's departure at four o'clock.

Yona and Ruth Tiefenbrunner with Brunia and her brother, Yankel, on either side of Yona

Miriam saw to it that this girl, with her profound thirst for knowledge, could make up for lost time. She custom-tailored a program of specialized tutoring to help her reach her grade level. By the time she was fourteen, she graduated eighth grade with honors.*

The children kept pouring into the home in the aftermath of the war, children of all ages and all kinds of problems. But very soon, the children fell into an idyllic routine — school in the morning and wonderful afternoons spent enjoying the verdant fields surrounding the home. In the mornings, it was Miriam who saw to the girls' appearances — brushing their hair each morning, spending hours ironing their hair ribbons and mending any torn clothes so they looked just so. In the afternoons, she would march with the children through the rolling fields, each group bearing their own homemade banner, singing timeless Agudah songs. Their youthful voices rang out clearly in the hills, with Miriam as their leader. Her head held high, she would march proudly in toe with twenty charges in rows of two.

"*Zeidim helitzuni ad me'od u'miTorascha lo natisi...*" "*Ashreinu mah tov chelkeinu...*" "*Hineh mah tov u'mah na'im sheves achim gam yachad...*" These were top among her repertoire of songs. How accurately they de-

* Today Brunia, now Mrs. Bracha Biegeleisen, is an esteemed member of the Nshei Chassidei Belz community in New York, the mother and grandmother of a large, beautiful family, and a teacher of Holocaust studies.

Miriam, seated in the center, surrounded by the girls she loved

fined Miriam's achievements. Miriam guided the remnant of children who had been spared from the claws of the evil Nazis, to embrace the Torah. How fortunate was their lot, how sweet were those wonderful times together!

She viewed each child in the home as her own child, and would come up with little things to brighten the days of the orphans and make them feel loved and cherished. She would take the time to photograph the children, fawning over their clothing and hair before she took the photos, because didn't all children deserve childhood photos to show their subsequent generations? After she developed them, she took special joy in handing them out to the children as keepsakes.

Indeed, Miriam conquered the hearts of the children — to their own advantage. She could get them to eat the most undesirable food, with her simple reassurances that it was delicious and healthy. More miraculous, perhaps, was her ability to get some of the children to open their mouths to pray.

Berek was the youngest of a partisan group. At only five years old, he had become "a man on the run," where pillaging was the key to survival. Berek's agenda did not include *berachos* or mitzvos. But his stubborn defiance was no match for the powerhouse named Miriam. How could he refuse to recite a blessing when this was the will of the woman who would take him roller skating?

Miriam coordinated and directed countless performances — dramas, choirs, and dances — allowing each child to shine. She produced a Chanukah play with the little ones, depicting Chanukah lights. With the older ones, she presented the poignant Yiddish song made famous by the chazzan Yossele Rosenblatt, "*Vos Vet Zein Ven Mashiach Vet Kumen*" (What will happen when Mashiach comes?). Miriam sewed the costumes herself. Aside from the entertaining aspect of her performances, she was instilling in the children an *emunah* and longing for the Redemption.

Each performance required numerous rehearsals, moments filled with the sounds of laughter and glee, hearts filled with confidence and

Miriam provided countless trips to the Land of Imagination...

Chanukah lights performance on Chanukah

Clown dance performance before Purim

Going "West" in an improvised nineteenth-century covered wagon. Miriam is on the right, holding a young child in her arms.

pride in their acting achievements.

Miriam's magic and charm inculcated nearly all the children — bereft of parents to guide them — with the fundamental character-development skills critical during those formative years. With her, they discovered friendship, loyalty, honor and self-respect, and obedience without subservience. And they learned to care about each other as naturally as breathing.

If the children didn't have parents, many at least had some kind of relative — an aunt, an uncle, a first or second cousin, who would visit periodically or keep in touch. But eight-year-old Renee and her nine-year-old brother, David, were utterly alone in the world; they had no surviving relatives.

With the elixir of compassion only her heart knew how to concoct, Miriam conveniently "discovered" that she was related to them. Is it possible to describe Renee and David's ecstasy and relief upon finding a relative as dear and precious to them as beloved Mademoiselle Miriam?

Miriam's good-natured, smiling presence and serenity were contagious. With radar-like precision, she intuited every child's deepest need, and she would do everything to soothe raw and sensitive emotions. In this way she succeeded in the herculean task of mitigating the children's pain and filling their inherent need for parental attention, love, and nurturing.

Miriam was so wildly successful that Monsieur assigned her the role of counselor to the twelve- and thirteen-year-old boys. She accepted the challenge, adapting perfectly to this new responsibility.

Her positive approach captivated the boys, restless with the edginess of pent-up emotions of grief and loneliness. And she kindled within

Miriam with her boys

them a genuine love of Torah and mitzvos. Little wonder that they held Miriam in the highest esteem and accorded her the deepest respect. Throughout the ensuing decades — to her dying day — the boys would maintain steady contact with her.

Aside from her work in the Tiefenbrunner Home, Miriam used her charm and tenacity to help rescue Jewish children from the gentile homes and institutions that had sheltered them during the war. She had many meetings with Mr. and Mrs. Moshe Swerdloff, emissaries of Agudath Israel Youth Council of America. The couple had been dispatched by Mike Tress, *zt"l*, Agudah's legendary leader, to bring back these children to their faith and heritage.*

Together with some of the older children who were fluent in French and Flemish, Miriam and the Swerdloffs would go on reconnaissance missions, traveling to the places where Jewish children had been identified as living. There they attempted to find out everything they could about the children's circumstances and, when possible, befriend them.

The next step was to approach the children's guardians. This was no simple endeavor, and Miriam was not beyond snatching these souls

* See *They Called Him Mike*, 272–368.

from those unwilling to release them to their people.

In 1949, Miriam left the home to marry a man whose giving nature mirrored her own. He was Gedalia Zupnick, a close disciple of Rav Chaim Shmulevitz, *zt"l*, who had spent the war years with the Mirrer Yeshivah in Shanghai. A native of Frankfurt, Germany, he was the son of Rabbi Avraham Menachem Zupnick, a Boyaner chassid from Poland.

Yankel Singer recalls feeling terrible disappointment when he learned the news that she was leaving to get married. "I finally found a woman who cared for me. She spoke Polish and Yiddish, my native languages. She was always smiling and had an engaging, spunky personality — the life of the orphanage! I was devastated when she left. I felt that her husband took her away from us..."

The Zupnicks relocated to America, but Miriam only moved geographically; her heart remained forever connected to the youngsters she had made her own.

The young Zupnick couple settled in Dubuque, Iowa, where Miriam's husband worked as a *shochet*. They were blessed with four daughters and then moved to Kansas City, Missouri. In 1957, when their young family needed schooling, they went to New York. By then, quite a number of the *Kinderheim* children had settled in America. Reunions began, incredibly joyful and frequent.

Devoted as Miriam was to her own precious daughters, the *Kinderheim* children remained a part of her family's framework. Every letter and phone call she received from one of her former charges was a source of tremendous *nachas*. Endless thought and time were invested in Miriam's responses to her correspondents, which made them doubly cherished. Each and every word was read and reread numerous times, seriously considered and savored.

Yankel Singer would visit Miriam regularly, sometimes several times a week. She remained a mother figure to him through his teenage years, his marriage, and beyond. On Yankel's wedding day, Miriam could not attend, because she had been hospitalized for an emergency medical procedure. Yankel ached to share his *simchah* with Miriam. After his *chuppah*, he slipped out for a few moments to visit her at her bedside and receive her blessings.

The Zupnicks lived in Crown Heights for many years. In time, the four Zupnick daughters married. After so many years of giving to others, Miriam and her husband could now enjoy *nachas* truly their own.

As they advanced in years, their precarious health convinced the Zupnicks to move to Lakewood in order to be closer to their two married daughters living there. Their fragile health, however, did not make a dent in their infectious *simchas hachaim*. Their home continued to be a home for Torah scholars, and the calls and letters from the former residents of the *Kinderheim* continued to pour in.

Miriam and her husband managed to attend the wedding of their eldest grandchild in Antwerp. The spontaneous reception Miriam received was incredible — flowers and chocolate befitting a queen! Everyone was anxious to introduce their families to Miriam and her husband.

Even after Rabbi Zupnik was summoned to the heavenly court, Miriam continued to mother those who had always remained her children. She would tell those who visited her and were horrified by her weakened condition, "I take some candies (painkillers) and then I feel better!"

Miriam was too filled with a zest for life to allow it to be sapped from her. In a physical state where most people would not even dream of venturing out of the hospital, Miriam undertook a trip to Israel with her granddaughter. News traveled quickly, and the boys living there arranged a reunion with her.

The Miriam they encountered was a frail, elderly woman, her body ravaged by illness. But to them, she was still their shining angel, their mother, with a number tattooed on her arm and immortal kindness indelibly inscribed in her heart. And they greeted her as such.

She could not have hoped for a more fitting farewell.

The final farewell occurred on Rosh Chodesh Kislev 5763, when Miriam returned her pure soul to her Maker.

11

A Promise with No Expiration Date

In 1949, caught up in the euphoria and the surge of Jewish pride following the establishment of the State of Israel, the Belgian Jewish Committee decided to bring all the children in their children's homes to Israel. Yona, too, was active in this endeavor. To show that it was serious, the committee even began the construction of a building near Tiberias.

Yona insisted on receiving assurances in advance of the move that all his children would be able to remain together in Israel. Yona feared for his children's spiritual well-being, which he had labored extensively to cultivate. Who knew what would happen to them if they were placed in secular kibbutzim? But the Youth Aliyah officials obstinately opposed Yona's request, and the aliyah dream was never actualized. Yona decided to move the home to Antwerp instead, where the children could be part of the Orthodox Jewish community.

Initially, the home moved into an annex of the Yesodei Hatorah yeshivah. Later it moved into its own building on General Drubbelstraat Street, about three-quarters of a mile from the school. The children continued to attend Yesodei Hatorah, where Yona taught for a while.

Outside Yesodei Hatorah on Lge Van Ruisbroeck Street, where the home was temporarily located upon its move to Antwerp, 1949

At first, the boys davened at the nearby Agudah Beis Medrash on Shabbos; on weekdays and the *Yamim Noraim*, they conducted their own in-house minyan. Later, they davened in their own minyan on Shabbos and *yom tov* as well. Usually Monsieur was the *ba'al tefillah* and the *ba'al korei,* too, but he always arranged special *ba'alei tefillah* for the *Yamim Noraim*. For a time Rav Zalman Lehrer, *shlita*, currently the head of the Machzikei Hadas Kehillah in Antwerp, davened *shacharis* on the *Yamim Noraim.* And for thirteen years, the *ba'al mussaf* was the late Reb Yisrael Dranger, a Chortkover chassid. Reb Yisrael was a successful businessman who openly attributed his success in business to his davening with the Teifenbrunner children.

The Tiefenbrunner Home hosted many prominent guests over the years. While still in Mariaburg, in the beginning of 1948, the chief rabbi of Israel, Rav Yitzchak HaLevi Herzog, visited. The *mara d'asra* of the time, the late Rav Yaakov Chaim Rottenberg, originally from Poland, would visit frequently during the time the home was housed in the Yesodei Hatorah building. His father lived a few houses away from the school, so he found himself there often. And from time to time, Yona would invite important guests to the *seudah shelishis* to give the boys much-needed *chizuk* and encouragement. Some of the guests included Reb Yankel Freidrich, a Lubavitcher chassid, a *talmid chacham,* and a great orator, who is now a distinguished member of Chabad in Antwerp. Another occasional guest was Rav Shalom Dovid Horowitz, a *talmid* of Chachmei Lublin Yeshivah, a Gerrer chassid, and one of the leaders of Agudath Israel of Antwerp.

Phillip and Henny Tiefenbrunner

There were also weekly Shabbos guests: Yona's brother Phillip (Pesach) and his wife, Henny, and their two children, Yechiel Efroim (Charlie) and Maggy. They lived within walking distance, and, as Maggy (now Mrs. Maggy Kompel) recalls, "we visited every Shabbos afternoon!" The weekly visits contributed a sense of extended family to the orphans who had no family nearby. Phillip and Henny also filled in for Yona and Ruth on the rare occasions when they took a few days' vacation.

Unlike staff members who came and went through the years, only Monsieur remained with the war orphans throughout, until the home's closing in 1960. His private office was often empty. The best place to find him was among the children — he was always circulating, providing subtle guidance where needed, singling out the ones who needed his attention most. Miriam Licht, who came to the home at the age of fifteen in 1949, remembers her first meeting with Monsieur.

"This is a family," he explained. "This is a home where all of the children are there for one another and feel a kinship with each other — always remember that. If you see that one of the children here need help, always give what you can, and if you ever need help, you can be sure you will receive as much as you need."

Miriam did need a lot of help. In 1940, her family — her parents and younger sister — had fled Antwerp, seeking refuge from the Germans in France. But in 1941, the Vichy government caught up with them, deported her father for forced labor, and subsequently sent him to Auschwitz. Miriam was only seven years old, but her grieving mother cast her into the role of an adult, burdening her with tremendous responsibility as the older of the two children.

They survived the war and returned to Belgium. Miriam's mother placed her younger daughter in the Tiefenbrunner Home, but Miriam could not go. She was very ill with tuberculosis and spent a year in quarantine before she was sent to join the Tiefenbrunners.

Miriam was fifteen years old at the time, but how she yearned to be a child still! Ever since her father had been ripped away from her, she hadn't had someone to lean on, someone to coach her, someone to father her.

"Mr. Tiefenbrunner took me under his wing and watched over me, cared about me," says Miriam. "He gave me security and self-confidence. Again and again, he would tell me that there's nothing I couldn't be! He made me feel like a princess!"

Furthermore, Monsieur helped her restore her *emunah,* which had been severely shaken when she learned that she would never see her father again. For years she refused to relinquish the hope of his return, and when the bitter realization dawned, she didn't think she could go on. With his warmth and sweetness, his willingness to listen, his positive reinforcement, Monsieur became the father she never really had.

When Miriam had arrived in the home, she had been attending Bnei Akiva groups. The Tiefenbrunner Home belonged to the Agudah movement, and the Tiefenbrunner children did not participate in Bnei Akiva. But Monsieur, ever attuned to the individual needs of every child, decided that Miriam could continue so long as she would not share the details of the meetings with her peers in the home.

Today, as an adult living in Israel, Miriam is a community activist with a reputation for her ironclad determination to help others. "People ask me," she says, "how I have the self-confidence to persevere, to let nothing stop me, where others are daunted. I owe it all to Mr. Tiefenbrunner. These are the legacies he endowed me with: you can be everything you want to be, and always see whom you can help."

Marian Katz received the same legacy: see what you can do for others. This lesson was driven home when Yona found out about the children and the bakery owner.

Marian came to the home after the war with her three siblings, ages 5, 3, and 2. The children used to walk to school every day, and because the regular route entailed passing by certain neighborhoods where gentile youths would shout anti-Semitic slurs, and even threaten to beat them, they looked for a detour. Going along some side streets, they passed a kosher bakery with a wonderful assortment of pastries, cookies, and cakes displayed in the shop window. Twice each day, as they passed the bakery, they would stop at the display window and press their noses against the glass, the delightful aromas and the sight of the delectable treats overwhelming their senses. How their mouths watered for a taste of those treats! The owner, feeling sorry for the orphans, would invite them in and share some pastries with the sizable group.

Some weeks later, Mr. Tiefenbrunner bumped into the bakery owner, who casually mentioned that he had regards from Yona's "children," who visited him daily. That evening, Monsieur approached Marian, as the oldest, and asked her to steer the group toward a different route so as not to pass the bakery anymore. He gently explained to her that the baker was struggling to make a living selling his wares, and by making him give away his merchandise, they weren't helping him any.

To this day, Marian follows the lesson Mr. Tiefenbrunner imbued her with: look over your shoulder and see what you can do for others.

When a child needed special medical care, it was Yona who personally accompanied him or her to the doctor's office. There was always a special treat on the way home: a can of soda (a rare treat in those days) or a visit to the fancy shops. Bracha Biegeleisen recalls that when she arrived at the home straight from Bergen-Belsen, a blistering rash covered her entire body. Monsieur insisted on personally taking her to the dermatologist several times to have it treated. This predated antibiotics, and the treatment was a painful procedure: soaking in a hot bath for a half-hour, brushing open the pustules to remove the pus, and finally applying a stinging sulfur ointment. The entire process left Bracha in great agony. On the way home, Yona would take her to a children's amusement center showing a film — *Bambi* or *Pinocchio* — which she greatly enjoyed, totally forgetting her discomfort.

Yona masterfully wove a rich Jewish atmosphere into the home's environment. To this day, the tunes and the Yekkish pronunciations of Yona's *zemiros* resonate with many of the children.

The children would often bring friends and neighbors home with them. In time, the home became a meeting place for many other *frum* young people who felt magnetically drawn, like a bee to nectar, to this enclave of warmth, where they imbibed nourishment for their souls.

On countless Shabbosos, these neighborhood children would come for the *oneg Shabbos* and Monsieur's *shmuessen* at *seudah shelishis.* Mostly he addressed the very fundamental concepts of the importance of Shabbos observance and the prohibition of consuming nonkosher foods. This was an accurate barometer of the spiritual challenges facing youth at this time, since most had spent the recent war years in environments estranged from *Yiddishkeit*. The catastrophic events and perils of the war had often resulted in situations of *pikuach nefesh*, where Shabbos and even kashrus had to be compromised. Now, in the postwar era, where the urgency of *pikuach nefesh* no longer generally applied, it was important to reenforce and revalidate these two fundamental mitzvos.

Joseph Schreiber was among the neighborhood youth who joined the minyan for the Shabbos *shacharis* and *minchah* prayers, and soon he became the regular *ba'al korei*. Joseph's parents had befriended Yona years earlier, when he arrived in Belgium in 1939 and helped cover Yona's wedding expenses. At the onset of the occupation, Joseph and his parents escaped to a remote region in the south of France. He and his mother (his father had been killed) returned to Antwerp after the war. Now Joseph grew deeply attached to Yona, viewing him as a father figure and visiting him often. In a twist of *hashgachah pratis*, the families became related years later, when Joseph married Yona's second daughter, Judith.

Yona's selfless dedication wasn't limited to his children's home. Mr. Yaakov Zamoire, currently one of the prominent *ba'alebatim* in Antwerp, was a contemporary of Yona's who lived in Brussels in the immediate aftermath of the war. Yona approached him soon after the liberation, extremely concerned about the Jewish education of the children in Brussels who had survived the war.

Like a father to a son, Yona with one of the Kinderheim boys

"Mr. Tiefenbrunner wanted me to become a teacher. I never dreamed of becoming a teacher!" When he saw that Yona practiced what he preached, that he was so concerned for the spiritual welfare of all Jewish children, becoming a teacher in Yesodei Hatorah on top of his duties involved in directing his children's home, Mr. Zamoire took the message to heart. He became more and more involved in teaching, eventually becoming a teacher of Jewish studies, a position he maintained until his retirement. Today Mr. Zamoire is still giving a *shiur* in Antwerp's old-age home.

Yona's heart was open to any and all children who needed a place to call home, under any circumstances. For the Reitzer children, theirs were happy circumstances that brought them to the *Kinderheim*.

The young Reitzer family lived in Schulen, a small picturesque village about an hour's drive from the Jewish community of Antwerp. The Reitzers had married in Nazi-occupied France in 1942, and through a series of miracles, they had escaped the Gurs detention camp in France and remained in hiding for the duration of the war. Following the war, the Reitzer family settled in Schulen. When the children reached school age, the closest yeshivah was Antwerp's Yesodei Hatorah school, too far for the children to commute each day. The answer was the Tiefenbrunner Home in Antwerp.

In 1951, seven-year-old Fanny Reitzer entered the Tiefenbrunner Home, where she boarded for the next five years until she graduated Yesodei Hatorah's eighth grade. Until the home's closing in 1960, three more Reitzer children would call the *Kinderheim* their home away from home.

"We weren't like the others," reminisces Faigy. "We had parents who could visit us; we had a real home to return to for the *yamim tovim*. We even had a grandmother in France — my companions in the *Kin-*

Yona and Ruth Tiefenbrunner with their three daughters, 1952

derheim couldn't fathom having grandparents. The orphans had no parents, much less grandparents! Still, Monsieur cared for us with as much devotion as the others."

The Reitzer parents would come to visit periodically, and thus began the friendship between them and the Tiefenbrunners, including Yona's brother and sister-in-law, Phillip and Henny.

Perele Kaszovitz, Faigy's younger sister, became very close to Yona's youngest daughter, Mariette, ties they still keep. She cannot forget how Mr. Tiefenbrunner cared for the children.

Both sisters, Faigy and Perele relate that when they visit their mother's grave in the Jewish cemetery near Antwerp, they also go to Yona's nearby grave, an expression of their deeply entrenched *hakaras hatov*.

"He has an ordinary *matzeivah* (tombstone)," says Faigy, "and every time I go there, I think, *Leeba G-tt, vos der Yid hut oifgetohn — Dear G-d, what this Jew has accomplished, if only the world knew!*

Much effort was invested in establishing traditions to give the children a sense of family. The backyard was filled with roller skates, balls, jump ropes, and other games. Every Sunday the children would go to see a presentation at the children's theater which offered wholesome, child-appropriate films. On Chanukah, the children would draw lots, each receiving a friend's name for whom they were given an allowance to purchase a special gift. There was also a grab bag gift, and a gift from the *Kinderheim* to the children. So many gifts — the *Kinderheim* children's Yesodei Hatorah classmates were jealous! For Pesach, everyone received new suits and dresses. And come summertime, Mr. Tiefenbrunner would take the children to the Ardennes Mountains, where he rented a chateau, a rooming house nestled on a hill. They traveled by train from Antwerp, which delivered them right to the entrance of the chateau.

The chateau by the river in the village of Anseremme (located in the Ardennes Mountains), where the Tiefenbrunners spent many summers with the children of the home

The breathtaking scenery, where tree branches interlaced the vast stretches of cloudless sky, was pure therapy for the children. They left behind the harshness of both cement and the realities of their lives, and, senses heightened, reflexes relaxed, they reveled in the wonders of the carefree, nonacademic surroundings.

The Tiefenbrunners took full advantage of the chance to give the children a fun time. In the river nearby, Monsieur would take the children boating and teach them to swim. He had a Harley Davidson motorcycle and would offer the children rides. Once a week the Tiefenbrunners took the children on meticulously planned excursions, lasting from early morning till late evening. They would hike down mountain trails, enjoy boat rides, swim, have picnic lunches on grassy knolls, and then head back to camp drunk with blissful fatigue.

On one such excursion, the boys made some exciting discoveries: guns and other pieces of artillery strewn about. They were relics of the not-too-distant past: the Ardennes Mountains, situated on the border between France and Belgium, had been the site of the Battle of the Bulge, the final German counteroffensive at the end of World War II.

The laid-back atmosphere of those weeks of summer reprieve made for many wonderful lifetime memories. The davening and learning were somehow sweeter and more precious in the serene tranquility. Shabbos, too, was special. With all the children casually spread out on the lawn,

Daily learning with Mr. Tiefenbrunner at the resort, 1959

Yona would teach the weekly chapter of *Pirkei Avos*.

Thus, many winters and summers passed, and the children blossomed into young adulthood.

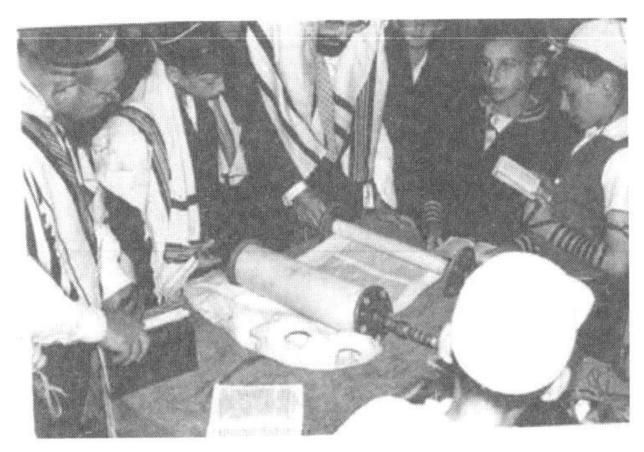

Davening with krias haTorah at the resort

Besides giving them a sense of family, Yona did what any father must do for his children: he did his utmost to guide each child toward a profession so that none of them would leave the home without a secure means of living. After completing high school, some children attended the School of Commerce in Antwerp, after which they were apprenticed to various trades.

The dining room at the resort

Some of the boys continued their learning by entering the hallowed study halls of the few western European yeshivos that existed in the 1950s. One address was the Eitz Chayim yeshivah in Koeppel, Belgium, founded by the now-centenarian *rosh yeshivah*, Rav Yitzchok Dov Koppelman, *shlita*, in 1946. Another was the yeshivah in Lucerne, Switzerland, then under the leadership of Rav Moshe Soloveitchik. Others attended the yeshivah in Gateshead, England, founded in 1942 by the Torah luminary of England, the Lithuanian-born Rav Eliyahu Dessler, *zt"l*.

Most of the children lived in the Tiefenbrunner Home until young adulthood, between the ages of eighteen and twenty-five, during which time they had begun working. Many of the boys entered the flourishing diamond industry in Antwerp, while the girls taught or worked as secretaries in the diamond industry.*

Yona never knew how long the children would remain in his care. Some were claimed by their family members eventually, after several years. Not all of the children left the home willingly. The home was their happiness, their security. Often the parents who reclaimed their children remained bitter and depressed, their home environments bleak. The children longed for the sweet days spent in the company of friends, under the warm guidance and direction of Monsieur. Some, so filled with the longing, would even steal back into the yard after school to pretend for a few brief moments that they belonged!

As long as his children stayed, Yona was committed to raising them as Torah Jews with his entire heart and soul. His was a promise with no expiration date.

* Antwerp, nicknamed "the Diamond City," had been an on-again, off-again center of diamond trade since the 1500s, with the diamond cutters predominantly Jews. Diamond cutting had been known as a Jewish vocation from medieval times, since the cutting of polished diamonds was one of the few crafts in which Jews were permitted to participate by the medieval guilds of Europe. As of 1940, up to 80 percent of Antwerp's Jews were involved in the diamond trade.

With the onset of World War II in 1939, many Antwerp diamond dealers fled. Following the war, Antwerp's diamond industry saw a resurgence, and the Antwerp Jewish community quickly established an influential and highly successful stake in it.

12
Always His Children

With many of the orphanage children now supporting themselves from the local diamond industry, they could live on their own. Some married shortly after they left the home. How Yona rejoiced in their *simchahs*, each one like his own child! Whenever circumstances dictated, he would raise funds to help cover the wedding expenses and get the couple settled.

Clara,* one of Yona's "children," had originally come from a nonreligious home. When she got married, Yona begged her to keep a kosher home, but she refused, saying that kosher food was expensive. Yona took money from his own pocket and offered to give her a steady stipend to cover the cost of the food. But she would have none of it.

Many years later, a Tiefenbrunner companion of Clara's had occasion to meet her. They got to chatting, and Clara related that she had recently *kashered* her kitchen since her grandchildren were yeshivah boys and they wouldn't eat in her home.

Apparently, Mr. Tiefenbrunner's passionate devotion to *Yiddishkeit* — as exhibited by his negotiations with Clara — wasn't completely lost. If his pleas and prayers didn't impact Clara, perhaps they were redi-

---

* Name has been changed.

rected and had a part in bringing her children and grandchildren back to Torah.

The children who had married and settled nearby in Antwerp would come to visit. And when they had children of their own, they would bring their little ones to sit on Yona's lap. Neither the span of years nor geographical distance separated Yona from his children. They were his forever, far or near.

In 1948, Bessi Sturm, who lived with Monsieur since 1942, was now eighteen years old and living on her own in a rented room in Brussels. She would commute every day to Antwerp, where she worked for a diamond setter. Then she contracted tuberculosis, a disease that ran rampant among survivors at the time due to the malnutrition that so many had suffered during the wartime food shortages. She was recovering in a sanatorium in Davos, Switzerland,* when she met her husband-to-be, Meilich Mittelman, a young man also recovering from tuberculosis after surviving three years in Auschwitz.

Bessi wrote to Yona informing him of her plans to marry. He purchased a train ticket and traveled to Switzerland the very next day. Though Bessi had already left the home, she was one of his girls, and he deemed it imperative to meet with her prospective groom.

With a gleam in his eye, Meilich Mittelman fondly recalls the meeting with the man who portrayed himself no differently than any father would.

For years, his numerous daily obligations notwithstanding, Yona carved out time to maintain a steady mail correspondence with many of the children who had moved abroad. He personally wrote each letter — sometimes several pages long — to inquire about their personal lives and share news of their "siblings." How much pride he took in his children's milestones and achievements!

What stands out markedly among these letters are his trademark dry humor as he addressed sensitive issues and expressed his genuine

* Switzerland had many sanatoriums, since it was believed that clean mountain air was the best treatment for lung diseases.

concern for his children — conveying across continents a warm handclasp of oft-needed encouragement.

Bracha Biegeleisen had left the home in 1949. Her father had remarried, and she and her brother emigrated with him to America in 1951. Eight years later in 1957, she was getting married. A few days prior to her wedding, she received a letter from Monsieur.

"I wish I could be there," he wrote, "but have no assistant in the home to take over in my absence, so I will have to be content with writing.

"My girl, you have spent a good portion of your youth growing up here in a place with so many types of children. Your character and love for *Yiddishkeit* shone through and was to the satisfaction of everyone here and to myself as well.

"Upon your marriage, may Hashem protect you and give you His blessings. May your marriage be successful, with lots of *mazel.* My best regards to everyone, to your family and your husband-to-be! Heartfelt *mazel tov* wishes, Yona."

Leibush (Leon) Lipschutz and his sister had been in the Tiefenbrunner Home on Rue des Patriotes in Brussels during the war. Their older siblings — five brothers — had been deported. Their parents, who had managed to survive in hiding, returned to retrieve them and brought them to America in 1948. After settling in New York, Leon and Yona struck up a correspondence.

October 24, 1948

Mr. Leon Lipschutz
552 West 163 Street
New York 32

Dear Leon,

Thank you so much for writing to me. I was very happy to receive your letter. I understand very well how difficult it must have been for you until you became accustomed to life there. The distance and the difference in living conditions are not easy to overcome.

We have now about sixty kids at home. You are not familiar with the majority of them. Most of your friends have either moved to Eretz Yisrael or to America in the meantime, or they are located with families in Belgium, for example, Pardes. Kurt Dressler travels to America next week and perhaps will visit you there.

Next week, twenty-two of our children are going to Eretz Yisrael, under [the supervision of] Jessy Feldmann and Ms. Binchen Gelbert.

I hope to hear from you again soon. In the meantime, wishing you warm regards.

J. Tiefenbrunner

---

22 Lge.v. Ruusbroecstr.
Antwerpen
March 22, 1949

To: Mr. L. Lipschutz
552 West 163 Street
New York 32

Dear Leibische,

I am writing to you today regarding some concern: You know that little Willy was staying with us at the home.* I would like to know if a memorial date for his father was set and what that date is. Forgive me if perhaps by asking this I am agitating old wounds, but for the sake of the child it is important to know.

I have been back from Eretz Yisrael for two weeks now, where I visited all the children from our old *chevrah* (group). I must tell you, my heart swelled when I saw them. Thank G-d, they all have developed so well. Each one is a better *Jied* than the other. All

* Willy is Leon Lipschutz's nephew, his brother's son.

the *bachurim* are sitting and learning: Nathan, Manfred, Charles, Gaby, and so on, and the girls are in the kibbutz and are already partly *ba'alebustes* or are becoming that soon. Helga had a Purim wedding. Steffy has already been married for a while, and Rachel will have a Shavuos *chasunah*. When will we hear something of that sort from you?

Please let us hear back from you soon. Otherwise your reply will not reach us here in Belgium, but rather in Eretz Yisrael. We are planning to depart from here in a short while (three to four months).

In the meantime, many heartfelt wishes.

Yours,
J. Tiefenbrunner

J. Tiefenbrunner
22 Lge.v. Ruusbroecstr.
Antwerpen
May 5, 1949

Mr. L. Lipschutz
552 West 163 Street
New York 32

Dear Leibische,

This time your letter was written in great detail and arrived just in time for our yearly gathering in May. This year, the number was smaller. There were only David Sztroch, Henri Mozelsio, Freddi Zamoire, Fredi Villenbaum, the brothers Meizeles, the Rothchild kids, the two Grau sisters, and Edith Gruenewald (married) Bronnen. Eva Mozelsio's engagement was precisely on the day of our reunion. They are the ones who stayed in Belgium.

I've just noticed I changed my writing into French. It doesn't matter, though. You will understand anyway.

Natan is in Kibbutz Netiva in Gedera and will be very happy to receive your letter. When you want to learn how hard it is to study after a day of work, you should ask the guys in Eretz Yisrael. They can tell you all about it.

We have invited some of the old boys [from Rue des Patriotes] for Pesach. Joseph Adler and some others were our guests. It was really very homey, and from time to time, I thought of our Seder on Rue des Patriotes. But after all, I can tell you it was better then, because the *chevrah* today is more mixed, and the home to them doesn't have the same meaning as it had for us at the time.

A detailed letter from Avrum Tenenbaum arrived today. He has already been serving in the military in Eretz Yisrael for a while. He writes to me about the difficulties of keeping kosher and the halachos. He takes good care of himself. One can see in him how a kid who comes from a completely nonreligious family can turn into such a man.

Let us hear from you again soon, and send my best regards to your parents.

From yours,
J. Tiefenbrunner

July 24, 1949

Mr. Leon Lipschutz
552 West 163 Street
New York 32

Dear Leon,

I realize our summer vacations are at the same time as in America. Our kids are also having their vacation from July 5, and both homes, that is to say, Antwerp and Brussels, are residing in the Ardennes. We have a house here, which is wonderfully located and has every advantage: swimming (in the river), which is about fifty meters (about 55 yards) away from the house; the forest is directly behind us, and the air is fabulously fresh. Our place is completely isolated; there are no towns or villages for 3 km. around us, so our kids can run wild as much as they want to. Your little nephew is also with us.

I am surprised that you weren't informed about Radzik's journey. Don't you have any contact with friends here in Belgium, in Brussels or Antwerp, anymore?

Some of the older children are now in America: Helmut Hochman and his sister, Manfred (Maurice) Krollik, the two Hartmann brothers (Sigi is now a soldier in Germany), Kurt Dressler, and others.

In Eretz Yisrael are: Albert Tenenbaum, the Kirschbaum brothers and sisters, the two Sommers, Steffi, Binchen Gelbart, the Ehrentreus, both Amsels, Anna Cukier, and many more. Until now, the following have gotten married: first Steffi, then Helga, and now Rachel Kirschbaum, as well as Israel Ehrentreu. As you can see, the kids are growing and are getting married.

Avrumche is still in the military, but his release will be soon. Back then he traveled on his own, as he didn't feel well received at the home, firstly because of his Jewish outlook and secondly due to his trip to Eretz Yisrael.

Otherwise there isn't any other news. Sending many warm regards to you and your parents.

Yours,
J. Tiefenbrunner

Orphanage near the united communities
Antwerp
March 23, 1950

My dear Leibush,

Our letters must have crossed in the mail with the response to the invitation card and I hope it arrived on time. I perfectly understand that you are all busy now with the festivities of your sister's marriage and the guests you will be hosting during the *sheva berachos*.

Avraham Tenenbaum is not the only one to have problems. For example, Joseph Adler also has worries because he wants to get married this year, and he doesn't have money and the papers he needs to leave and to establish himself. I could continue to give you other examples that would show you how each of the older boys has his own concerns.

For your next letter, keep our new address so that the letter should arrive to us directly.

With my best wishes for a kosher Pesach,
B'virkas chag same'ach,
J. Tiefenbrunner

9.31.50

Dear Leibush,

Thank you for the card you sent. I wish you also from myself *gemar chasimah tovah.*

I wish you would reconsider what I wrote you once, but about which you didn't answer me yet.* I'm sorry if the question is difficult for you, but this is one of the things you have to do without paying attention to your feelings.

You know that here in Europe, either a *yahrtzeit* has been fixed or an approximate day for all people who didn't come back. And I think even further, after all, Willy's mother is not so old, and she could maybe remarry, and we also want to establish which day Willy should recite Kaddish.

Don't be upset with me if I ask you the question so brutally, but I ask now in the interest of the child.

I hope that you feel well, and that your whole family is fine.

In the meantime, I wish you all the best and wait for your news.

Yours,
J. Tiefenbrunner

---

* Mr. Tiefenbrunner is addressing the concern about Leon's older brother, who was presumed dead, but they never discovered the exact date and details. His son Willy, Leon's nephew, was living at the home at this time.

Dec. 3, 1950

Dear Leon:

Time and patience, I must tell you, are two things I do not really have. In any case, I am answering your letter because this is a link between the past and present. You can believe me, despite all the material hardships and dangers of those times, we had a closer relationship with the children. If not for the risks and the war, I would almost like to go back to those times...

Your little nephew Willy is learning very well and is very smart. He feels very good with us and would very much enjoy if you would write him a letter from time to time. It can be in Yiddish, English, or German. We will translate it for him.

Regards to your parents.

Yours,
Yona Tiefenbrunner

Jan. 13, 1951

This time I am a little late with my answer, but with the days of Chanukah approaching, you know there's always a lot going on with preparation for the party and the plays.

In any case, after all, let me wish you a hearty *mazel tov*! May The Creator bless your sister, and may your parents see much *nachas*! You wrote me that the *chasan*'s name is Leidner. Is he from the Karlsbrucher Leidners or is he Hungarian? Because the name sounds Hungarian.

Meanwhile, Mademoiselle Miriam, whom you perhaps know, went to America. If you don't know her, you certainly know her husband, Gedalia Zupnick. Your dear father knows his family well.

We are moving now to a different house, and your nephew

will probably join us... Otherwise, there is not too much news and hope to hear from you soon.

With our best regards,
Yours, Yona

March 20, 1951

Dear Leibush,

I really feel bad to have read that your parents are not in good health. I hope that their situation has improved and that it doesn't cause you any more concern. Anyway, *mazel tov* for the demobilization. With all the patriotic sentiments, we have to be aware that for us here the life of soldiers is not ideal, as is already the case in Israel, even where there is a whole Jewish army.

You write me that you changed your job. What's your job now? You also wrote to me that Nathan Kirschbaum got engaged. You forgot to write to me who is his *kallah*! Johnny Ansbacher and his brother Felix both got married in Eretz Yisrael. You see how it goes quick there?

Your nephew, Willy, is well and sends his best regards to you. I heard that he got a birthday present from his grandfather, and he's very thrilled with it.

You don't have to be surprised that there is not a minyan in the *beis midrash* in New York. It's not an exception — everywhere is the same thing. During the week, it's difficult to have minyan, even here in Antwerp. Certainly in the big synagogues, there is a minyan.

For today, I end with the hope to hear news from you.

Best regards,
Yona Tiefenbrunner

Orphanage near the united communities
Antwerp
July 2, 1951

Dear Leo,

About Willy, you do not have to worry. The boy is well developed and quite intelligent...

You probably know that Nathan Kirschbaum is married, as are most of your friends besides for the Amsel boys. We don't hear anything from you either!

Lately a large amount of children left for the U.S. Maybe you could meet? Mendel Landau is a Bobover chassid and davens by the Rebbe. Then you have the Schiowitz children and the Kohn child. When you meet one of them, they will tell you how everything looks here.

Best regards. I expect a letter from you!

Yours,
Yona Tiefenbrunner

Feb. 27, 1952

Dear Leibush and Mrs. Lipschitz,

I waited with my letter, because I wanted Wolf (Willy) to write to you as well. But now he went to his mother for Shabbos and said that he would write from there.

I see that you, too, want to be *mekayeim* the mitzvah of learning because you are learning with other people. It is only sad that the youth in America don't embrace Torah ideals en masse. Let us hope that in future times, the amount of religious Jews doesn't diminish and with that the influence of religious life in Israel. You cannot imagine how much this affects me, especially now, as I am preparing to move to Israel.

There are boys from us in school in Brooklyn who write me that the schools are very good, but it seems to me that there is a lack of *Yiddishkeit*. What are these schools actually like?

Now, before Pesach, I wish you a *freilichen* and *kasheren Pesach*.

Yours,
Yona Tiefenbrunner

Antwerp
September 4, 1952

Mr. Leon Lipschutz
552 West 163 Street
New York C 32

Dear Leo,

I am not sure if I already replied to your last letter. I'm organizing my correspondences during my vacation here, so I'm not sure anymore.

The school system doesn't really seem to have high standards, at least pertaining to what is called "yeshivot"... I am, of course, excluding the *chassidish* yeshivos from this rule, which are accomplishing good work. I ask myself only if this work is also indicative of life in the whole country in general. After all, the size of the American Orthodoxy is proportionally not much bigger than in other countries, and they surely don't have more influence. Or am I mistaken?

You mention an article from the morning newspaper. The writer of the article is biased and therefore not well qualified. On the other hand, it is only natural that an Agudist writer is not writing about the "*tachkemoni*,"* since every person sees life through his own glasses and will try to influence people to see his view.

Mazel tov upon receiving your American citizenship, but do you also have to serve military duty?

---

* Hebrew for "wise counselor."

For the forthcoming Rosh HaShanah, I wish you already now best wishes and that this year will bring the *geulah* for which we are all waiting.

Best and heartfelt wishes to your whole family.

Yours,
J. Tiefenbrunner

P.S. How old are you? Can we talk to you about a *shidduch*?

Antwerp
December 12, 1953

Mr. Leon Lipschutz
552 West 163 Street
New York C 32

Dear Leibish,

First of all, a warmhearted *mazel tov* on your engagement, and it really should be with a lot of *mazel*. My wife who is from Fulda* — her family's name is Feldheim — knows the family of your *kallah* and wants to inform you that you have chosen well. By saying it, she likes to prove to me that it isn't a bad thing to marry a Yekke.

Now, regarding the previous letter I wrote to you concerning Willy. Practically, as the situation stands, I can't do anything to stop it. It is a judicial decision, which states that Willy will be given to his uncle in Montreal. The decision is prompted by the fact that the uncle was Willy's guardian before, and the uncle has a son at the same age as Willy and he lived together with him for a while, so Willy will have a friend his own age there and it will be easier for him to adjust to a new environment. It has been very difficult for me to press and arrange for him to first visit his grandparents and spend a few weeks there so that he can get to know them. Should there be any difficulties, if you are not agreeable with this decision, these options will disappear. I am writing this to you in a

* Fulda is a city in central Germany.

very frank way in order to avoid any misunderstandings, and you know that I am not someone who will want to delude you.

The visa was already granted earlier, but we still had to handle the court issues. Before the beginning of January the boy can't travel.

I implore you to immediately send a confirmation, by airmail express, that everything in the way that I wrote to you now is all right, so that there will not be any difficulties at the last minute.

I hope that your dear father is doing better now and he can go out. I wish him a *refuah sheleimah* and that he shall have *nachas* from his children.

Heartfelt blessings,
Yours,
J. Tiefenbrunner

December 28, 1953

Mr. Leon Lipschutz
552 West 163 Street
New York C 32

Dear Leibusch,

I would like to reply to your letter immediately to prevent any more mistakes and so that Willy's trip won't start under false premises. It has been unknown to us whether before our tribunal the mother, *aleha hashalom*, had set up a tribunal before court in which the brother Nathan was to be the guardian. There wasn't any copy or annotation in the paperwork. Later, though, the magistrate confirmed it according to the records and required of the new tribunal to agree with the previous guardian decision. Based on this, the matter developed differently than perhaps was clear in my first letter. In any case, we couldn't disregard the voice of the first guardian.

It goes without saying that the uncle in Canada will not allow under any condition for Willy to stay in New York. What I have accomplished, with great trouble — for Willy to come to you next — I could only achieve by giving my word of honor, promising Willy will further travel to Canada. Otherwise, the person would have proceeded against me in a court of law due to misuse of my guardian rights. This is the exact situation.

Henceforth, I thank you for your cooperation. The child will leave here on the 11th of January, and the day after will arrive by you. You can find out the exact arrival time at the travel agency.

Best and heartfelt wishes to all of you,
Yours, J. Tiefenbrunner

This is but a small sampling of the correspondence Yona kept with his children. Such fatherly love and concern did not, could not, go unreciprocated. The correspondence between Yona and his children who had emigrated to Israel and America flowed both ways. How Yona relished receiving mail from his children abroad! And Yona delighted in sharing the news with the "siblings" in the *Kinderheim*.

On countless Shabbos afternoons, Yona would gather the children, excited: he had a letter to share! Master storyteller that Yona was, the children would sit spellbound as Yona enthusiastically read line after line, inevitably injecting his humor. The children listening sensed the tangible bond that connected Yona to the letter's author; it mirrored the eternal connection that Monsieur had forged with each of them.

13

How Could the Heart that Beat for Others Stop Beating?

Twenty years had gone by since the Tiefenbrunner Home had come into existence, and now the last child was leaving. The Belgian Committee had decided that it was time to close the doors of the Tiefenbrunner Home.

There are degrees of sadness in the closing of doors. But Yona, whose sole life occupation had been caring for the children, was never the same after closing this chapter in his life.

At the reception for the closing of the home in 1960. Yona is in the center, sitting next to his brother Phillip.

The investment of his strength and energies — of the best years of his life — in caring for orphans had earned Yona his share of eternity in the heavenly realms. But it left him hardly any financial savings to live on and support his wife and daughters. He was offered no pension or retirement package by the Belgian Jewish Committee members, who had enjoyed great profits from the contributions that had come from America (from the AJC/Joint) over the years.

All this would have embittered a lesser man. Yona's heart was no longer in the best of health. As he had written to Bracha Biegeleisen in 1958, he was suffering from coronary disease — a "tribute to his work during the war," as he coined it — and had spent two months in a sanatorium to recuperate. Now the financial difficulties compounded the stress. But Yona, ever the consummate giver, could not conceive of taking.

During the next two years, he struggled for a way to support his wife and three daughters. So great was the daily financial strain that it exacted a heavy toll on his weakened heart.

At the young age of forty-eight, Yona's heart, which had always beat for others, stopped beating forever on September 15, 1962, the seventeenth of Elul 5722. This pure and gentle soul who had heroically fulfilled his life's mission in the most trying of circumstances, without personal gain or recognition, left this world unheralded.

Alas! Yona, the father of all the orphans whom he'd married off joyously, and the grandfather of their young offspring who had often come to visit him, would not dance at his own daughters' wedding or live to see the joys of grandchildren. The bitterness of this irony was the most painful pill to swallow for his daughters, Jeanette, Judith, and Mariette.

And because Yona was the ultimate paragon of "*hatznei'a leches*," of humility in greatness, the full story of the countless numbers of those whom he saved, and the majority of his legendary *mesiras nefesh* in saving *Yiddishe kinderlach* from the claws of the Nazi murderers, went with him to the grave.

The terrible news of Monsieur's premature passing spread like wildfire around the world to all the corners that Yona's children inhabited. Many were those who lit a *yahrtzeit licht* for him at the news, who cried bitter tears — to the bafflement of new spouses and families. They couldn't fathom the depths of the grief and loss they were witnessing, because they hadn't known who Monsieur really was to so many.

September 28, 1962

Dear Gertie and Leo:

I was very happy to receive your letter and to know that everything is fine in your family. You will certainly excuse me for not having written till now. I was just about to do it when nearly two weeks ago we had this terrible shock.

Leo, don't be sorry for not having known how things were. Mr. Tiefenbrunner, as I told you, was never the same again after he left the children's home. That was his only ideal, you know that. All these years, he earned some money he could put away, but nevertheless it wasn't too much. Most things he did, he did honorably. Two years ago he was employed as a bookkeeper in a Jewish firm that was just building up a new diamond-cutting factory. As one can't really make a living for a whole family as a bookkeeper, Mr. Tiefenbrunner put all his last pennies into this venture, as many other Antwerp people did.

It was very unfortunate, because not entirely a year passed by when this firm declared bankruptcy.

This gave him a bad stroke, which aggravated a heart condition, on top of a few other illnesses he had already. Many people at that time offered to help him, but he would never accept. He was just too good, always there for giving, never for taking.

After recovering somewhat, he got a job as a typewriter in a Jewish garment factory. As you can imagine, they had little to live on from that time on. He still didn't want to accept financial help.

As you wrote, I was really close to him, as were many, many other children who knew him. That unhappy night I was there, the same day he was at the office and felt no worse than any other ill person feels. It came suddenly in the evening. Fortunately, he didn't suffer.

There are so many here to miss him.

Yours,
Willy

True, the sun set at midday the day that Yona left this world. But Yona's light did not dim. Out of the ruins of European Jewry, Monsieur Tiefenbrunner had created a new generation of builders.

Around the Jewish world, half a century later, yeshivos, chassidic courts, and Jewish communities throughout the globe reap the rewards of Yona's investment in "his" children. Some of the most prominent *maggidei shiurim*, *rabbanim*, *ba'alebatim*, teachers, and mothers today are the spiritual children, grandchildren, and great-grandchildren of Yona Tiefenbrunner.

Yona's daughter Judith at her father's grave site

Epilogue
A Place among the Heroes of Our People

In a banquet hall in Jerusalem, on August 8, 2002, sits a group of close to one hundred people chatting and laughing. The emotionally charged air resonates with joyous expressions and shouts in several languages — French, Flemish, Hebrew, and English — as eyes meet and recognition dawns. Many of those present haven't seen each other in over forty years!

They are mature men and women from all walks of life. Once, long ago, they had been a disparate group of young troubled orphans, victims of a world gone mad, who'd been brought together by fate. When they went their own separate ways, they each had to look doggedly ahead, putting their burdened pasts behind them in the effort to find their own constructive life paths. Now they have chosen to come together once more, nearly half a century later, to collectively look back.

It is time to pay tribute to their common childhood hero and savior, Yona Tiefenbrunner, *zt"l*, upon the occasion of his fortieth *yahrtzeit*.

The idea had been simmering for some time. A group of Yona's "children" living in Israel who had maintained close ties through the years began compiling a list of invitees for the reunion. They began with the names of the ones who had stayed in touch over the years.

But there had been many others. They gathered a collection of photos, some of their own, many that were in the possession of Yona's daughters. They jogged their memories. Many faces were accounted for. Some weren't. Over two hundred children had lived in the Tiefenbrunner Home over the course of the twenty years between 1940 and 1960, but not all had been there at the same time. It was a laborious task trying to track everyone down. Where did they live now? Did they still go by the same names? In the case of the girls, what were their married names?

And then they wondered: Would anyone come? Would fear of creating emotional upsets cause reluctance to summon up the past? Could the silence of so many years be broken?

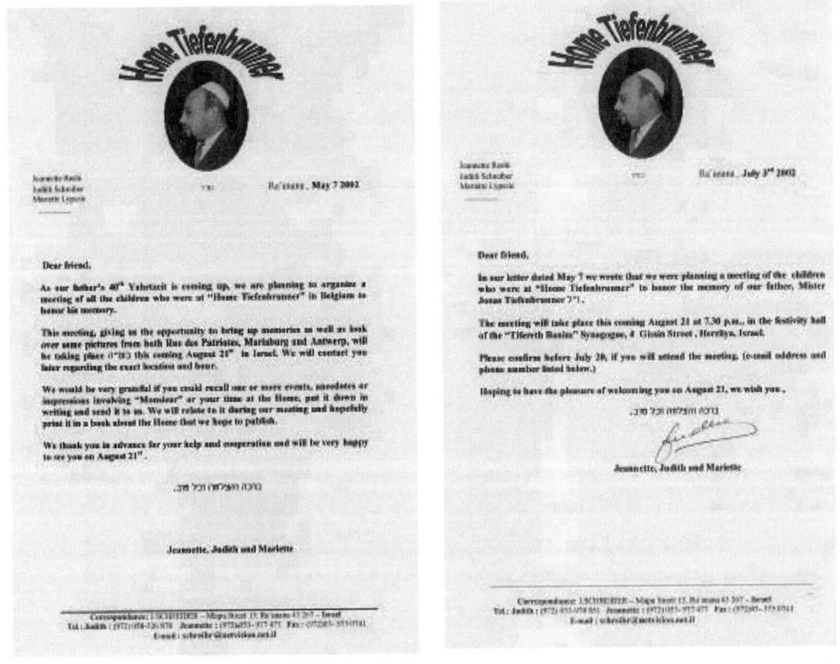

Home Tiefenbrunner

Ra'anana, May 7 2002

Dear friend,

As our father's 40th Yahrtzeit is coming up, we are planning to organize a meeting of all the children who were at "Home Tiefenbrunner" in Belgium to honor his memory.

This meeting, giving us the opportunity to bring up memories as well as look over some pictures from both Rue des Patriotes, Mariaburg and Antwerp, will be taking place this coming August 21st in Israel. We will contact you later regarding the exact location and hour.

We would be very grateful if you could recall one or more events, anecdotes or impressions involving "Monsieur" or your time at the Home, put it down in writing and send it to us. We will relate to it during our meeting and hopefully print it in a book about the Home that we hope to publish.

We thank you in advance for your help and cooperation and will be very happy to see you on August 21st.

ברכה והצלחה וכל טוב.

Jeannette, Judith and Mariette

Home Tiefenbrunner

Ra'anana, July 3rd 2002

Dear friend,

In our letter dated May 7 we wrote that we were planning a meeting of the children who were at "Home Tiefenbrunner" to honor the memory of our father, Mister Jonas Tiefenbrunner ז"ל.

The meeting will take place this coming August 21 at 7.30 p.m., in the festivity hall of the "Tifereth Banim" Synagogue, 4 Gissin Street, Herzliya, Israel.

Please confirm before July 20, if you will attend the meeting. (e-mail address and phone number listed below.)

Hoping to have the pleasure of welcoming you on August 21, we wish you,

ברכה והצלחה וכל טוב.

Jeannette, Judith and Mariette

Invitations to the reunion of the children of the Tiefenbrunner Home on the occasion of the fortieth yahrtzeit of Yona Tiefenbrunner

But come many of them did. And many of those who couldn't make it — living overseas or having prior commitments — sent sincere regrets along with written accounts of their memories and tributes to Yona Tiefenbrunner.

Few things have the power to pull at one's heartstrings as do memories of childhood. Sitting around those tables, catching up on each other's lives, they are magically drawn backward through the years. A flood of memories, alternately blissful and painful, come flooding back, and the tales of long ago begin gushing forth. Some details are crystal clear. Others are murky, faded by the sands of time. But the pieces all come together in the end. And when they have each exhausted their stories, they compare their own respective adult lives with that of Yona's.

At the fortieth yahrtzeit reunion

It comes to them then that Yona never experienced a private life of his own. He had lived entirely for them; he had sacrificed his family life so they could grow and thrive. Through mature eyes, a newfound sense of wonder and recognition of the man they called, simply, "Monsieur" emerges from the haze of decades past.

Kalman Jung (right) speaking to Maurice Tiefenbrunner (standing next to him on the left) at the fortieth yahrtzeit

Yona Tiefenbrunner, gone over forty years, deserves his rightful place among the heroes of our people in the annals of history.

Gift given to the participants of the gathering

Through a Child's Eyes

The true account of Aron Peterfreund

Through a Child's Eyes

Not a Holiday and Not a Picnic

Antwerp, May 16, 1940

"Yay! A holiday!"

Those were the first words out of my six-year-old lips that morning when Mamma informed me I wasn't going to first grade at yeshivah Yesodei Hatorah because we were going away. Peeking outside, I saw a lorry waiting outside the window.

"A trip!" I jumped up and down gleefully, thrilled at the prospect of a journey. A lorry unquestionably meant we were going on a trip. Our family did not own a car and we typically traveled everywhere by train. But the summer before, when our family had vacationed in Bruges,* Papa had rented a small truck to get us there.

"Where are we going this time?" I sang out innocently.

Neither Papa nor Mamma paid any attention to me. They were too busy rushing around.

---

* A historic city in northwest Belgium favored by tourists for its medieval architecture.

We didn't take any of our clothing, but we did take the pot with the stew cooking on the stove. Mamma asked me to carry it carefully into the lorry and hold it on my lap. I knew she was going to have a baby soon, and she had begun counting on me, quite often taking me shopping with her so I could help her carry home the bags.

We piled into the lorry — Papa, Mamma, my four-year-old sister, Eva, and myself — and headed out. "A picnic?" I asked hopefully.

Before I could expect an answer, I was distracted by the scene on the road.

"Look!" I cried. "A parade!"

The road was choked with traffic, cars, and trucks all headed in the same direction.

"Why are the so many cars on the road? Where is everyone going and are we going there, too?"

I plied Papa with question after question. But Papa's eyes remained fixed on the road, his lips curved in a look of intent concentration.

We had not gone very far when suddenly we had to stop. In front of us were overturned wagons and the carcasses of dead horses blocking the road. In the distance, we could hear what sounded like loud thunder. And the crashing sounds were getting closer!

"What's happening ?" I yelled above the din.

Finally, Papa turned to me. "It's a war, Aron. The Germans have invaded our country, and they are supposed to be approaching our city today.

"They're raining down bombs to overcome our army," he whispered to me so as not to scare little Eva. Papa explained that everyone in the city was evacuating — a new word he had just taught me — to stay out of harm's way until the Germans had fully occupied Antwerp. We were going to cross the border into the neighboring area of France, which the Germans hadn't overtaken yet.

It would be a few days at most, he reassured me. As soon as the Germans had fully taken control of our city, we could go back home, and life would return to normal.

"They say there's no more room on the trains," Papa said. *Aha! So that's why Papa rented the truck!*

"Where we will stay?" I asked Papa.

He said that there were hundreds, maybe thousands, of people escaping, and the schools, the churches, they were opening their doors for us.

As we joined the queue of vehicles snaking their way across the border, I wasn't really afraid. I did not know I was supposed to be. The journey was rather exciting to my adventurous mind. I often fabricated heroic tales for my playmates, but this one was true and I will have starred in it. My mind raced. *I saw bombs! We made a daring escape and crossed the border!*

Innocent Encounters with German Soldiers

May 25, 1940

"To life! To safety! To *gezundt*!"

Two beer-filled glasses clinked together as my father playfully toasted...a German soldier!

Only a week after we had hastily fled our home, and sleeping in what I recall was a roadside monastery, we were headed back to Antwerp. We had heard that the Germans had triumphed over the Belgian army, and the city had quieted down. No one dreamed that the Germans would actually stay, that this illusion of calm was the onset of the annihilation of our people.

The late May sun beat down mercilessly; we were extremely thirsty. Presently we spotted a kiosk on the outskirts of Antwerp. What a relief! Papa treated us all to cold drinks. A German soldier sat at a table near ours. Oh! To think I was seeing a real live soldier with his fancy uniform!

My incessant stares attracted his attention. He smiled at us kindly, politely inquiring about the welfare of us small children, our rumpled unwashed clothing the telltale signs of refugees.

"Let's drink a toast to you and your family's safety and health!" he gallantly offered my father.

That was my first encounter with the Germans. It wasn't the last before I would radically alter my initially innocent opinion of them.

That fall, I was outside playing in the street. From afar I could see a German army jeep approaching. At that time, cars were not yet the widespread mode of transportation in our area, and while my six-year-old mind could compute the time it would take a horse and buggy to reach me, I had no way of calculating the speed of the moving vehicle. Casually I began crossing the street. Next thing I knew I was hit by the jeep, and although only mildly injured, I lay sprawled on the street in front of it.

The German driver and his companion lifted me gingerly and drove me to the hospital, where I received some stitches on my forehead. Later they came back to check in on me, bringing sweets for me, and fragrant, delicious bread and pastries for my parents in apology.

But my good opinion of the Germans did not last long.

The Germans Are Monsters!

January 1942

My childish romanticized illusions were rudely shattered by the arrest of our father late one Friday afternoon. We didn't know where he'd disappeared, but lately news was spreading that the Germans had begun arresting Jews at random. When Papa didn't come home in time for Shabbos that evening, the shock was horrifying. Did they really take Papa? A mournful Tishah B'Av–like atmosphere prevailed, silence replacing the usual *zemiros* Shabbos in our house.

On Shabbos morning, Mamma took me and my sister to the local Gestapo police office in Antwerp.

"How can we help you?" a Gestapo agent dressed in civilian clothing asked her politely.

"My husband! It's a mistake. He's innocent!" she screamed at them. She couldn't grasp yet that that she was dealing with people who had turned into animals, beasts thirsty for Jewish blood.

The Gestapo agent coolly tried to calm her down, addressing the problem with the same concern as for a stray kitten. Scorching tears stung my eyes as we walked away, dejected. How could an adult mock Mamma so? How could they completely disregard our concern about our father? And that's when I told myself: *Those Germans are all evil monsters!*

To our profound joy and relief, after Shabbos Papa came home! He had succeeded in jumping off a train whose destination we would later find out was the Mechelen transit camp, which forwarded its detainees to Auschwitz.

School Closes!

April 1942

I tried to immerse myself in the pleasant things of life. I loved going to yeshivah. I loved going to the Sanzer *shtiebel* with my father on Shabbos. Papa was a native of Nowe Sanz, Poland, and enjoyed the camaraderie of his *Sanzer landsleit*.

My father had been fifteen years old when he emigrated with his parents from Poland to Belgium in 1923. He married my mother, also Polish born, in 1933. Both of my parents had by then obtained Belgian citizenship.

My paternal grandparents lived nearby. How I loved the special attention my grandfather lavished on me! He would often invite me to join them for the Friday night *seudah*. I also enjoyed playing "big brother" to my two little brothers, two-year-old Moshe Leib (born in late 1940), and Oscar, an adorable toddler (born in 1941).

But trouble was brewing.

Right after Pesach, in the middle of a school day, we were told that the learning had to stop. The yeshivah was closing! No one explained anything to us. We were all sent home. The very young children were escorted in groups by the teachers to their homes to startled parents.

The Yellow Star

May 1942

Mamma sewed the now mandatory yellow star on all our coats. "Be careful!" she implored me each time I left the house. Wearing the yellow star disturbed me very much. I hated to be restrained from moving freely. With no school to attend, I used to love going out to visit friends, and I continued strolling about, not sensing any immediate danger.

We lived near a cinema, and often my grandfather would treat us to a film. Once, my sister Eva and I went to watch a documentary film of scuba divers showing wondrous deep-sea creatures. As I made my way in, I realized my annoying yellow star was falling off, so I ripped it off completely and threw it into the cellar nearby. I instructed Eva to take off her jacket as soon as we had entered.

I remember sitting in the dark, watching the intriguing film, when suddenly the lights went on. In burst German soldiers, looking for Jews! I sat very comfortably with my sister and didn't dare turn around. Being blond-haired and blue-eyed, the "Aryan advantage" now stood in my favor for the first time.

Soon enough, the film resumed as if nothing had happened.

Only the Ostjuden?

May 1942

The first time I saw a black van full of Jewish people passing me in the street, I waved them off. "Have fun!" I shouted after them. I loved traveling and had not learned of the dreaded word that before long was on everyone's lips: *deportation.*

This is how I found out how the black van translated into the tragedy unfolding in our midst:

One day soon after, Mamma and I were admiring something in a shop window. At the sudden sound of shouting, I lifted my eyes to the dreadfully terrifying scene happening across the street. *No! It couldn't be!* I didn't want to believe what I was seeing. I was praying that I had mistaken the home that was being raided. But I knew that apartment house in my sleep. It was the building of Moshe, my classmate and dearest friend.

German soldiers, with the help of sinister-looking Belgian youth shouting in Flemish (whom I later found out were called Flemish Blood Shirts because they collaborated with the Nazis) were brutally kicking and shoving beloved Moshe and his family into a waiting black van with the infamous Nazi skull-and-bones symbol.

It all happened in an instant, in the blink of an eye. Mamma and

I froze, unable to utter a sound as my mind tried to process the unbelievable. Why was his family being apprehended? Would I ever see him again? My fearful gaze traveled feverishly, for a fleeting moment catching Moshe's eye. Why didn't he react? Why did he quickly avert his eyes, as if he regarded me, his best friend — firing him a tear-filled farewell message — a total stranger?

All too soon, Mamma regained her wits. "Deportation!" she whispered to me. "He doesn't want the Germans to recognize you as his friend! Let's run!"

Young as I was, instinct had me turn quickly turn away from them so they wouldn't spot my yellow star. To further remove any trace of evidence that I was a Jewish boy, I quickly slipped the beret from my head, stuffing it into my pocket. Then I slithered away after Mamma, silencing the scream inside my throat.

Only the Ostjuden. They're only taking the Ostjuden. The recent Eastern European immigrants...Moshe's family were Romanian immigrants... Belgian citizens are safe.

That was what everyone was saying. I wasn't convinced.

The Shvartzer Shabbos

June 1942

Oh! The horrors of the *Shvartzer Shabbos*! We all called it the *Shvartzer Shabbos*, that black Shabbos that the Germans lured my dearest aunts, twenty-one-year-old Hendel Malka and sixteen-year-old Tzila, my father's younger unmarried sisters, and countless other young people, to their unsuspecting, brutal deaths in Auschwitz.

All single young men and women had been ordered to present themselves for work in Germany to assist in the war effort. They were to report to the central train station that Shabbos afternoon. It was unthinkable to refuse the order.

Since I often slept over at my grandparents on Friday night, I can vividly recall waking up Shabbos morning to the sight of my grandfather weaving Belgian francs deep into my aunt's thick hair in preparation for her journey. *Pikuach nefesh*, he muttered painfully again and again. They would need money once they reached their destination. And maybe the money could somehow buy them their freedom and their return home sooner.

I joined the mournful, slow procession that accompanied hundreds of brave young people to the station on Shabbos. The parting was tearful. We agonized over the hardship of the forced labor awaiting them, and we prayed that they return soon, safe and sound. Who could have imagined that they voluntarily and blindly went to their brutal deaths?

The group of young people never had to work. My two young aunts would be the first two of the twelve of my immediate family members who were cruelly murdered *al kiddush Hashem* in Auschwitz. Out of my extended family, of 160 Peterfreunds who originated from Poland in the 1890s, only seven would be left after the war.

My World Collapses

June 1942

"Now your name is Arnold, understand?"

Because of the hovering fear of deportation, Papa had contacted a gentile man, a member of the Belgian underground, who agreed to take in all of us children — myself, age 7, Eva, age 5, two-year-old Moshe Leib, and seventeen-month-old Oscar.

He and his family lived in Essen, a quaint village on the Dutch border. Officially, we went to the summer camp of the school in the village. Other than our host family, the two gendarmes of the village, and the nearest neighbors of our host family, all of whom were members of the Belgian underground, no one knew we were Jewish; I became Arnold, Moshe Leib became Leon.

I was enjoying the country air and the feeling of safety, far from the city that was now teeming with Nazi soldiers everywhere. My little brothers were too little to understand much. But Eva was miserably homesick.

"Take me back to Mamma!" she cried incessantly.

When the host family decided to send her back home for two weeks, her joy knew no bounds. After the two weeks had gone by, Josephine, one of the daughters of our host family, went to fetch Eva. As she approached our street, she noticed a big crowd standing opposite our house. The Nazis were arresting my family for deportation — Papa, Mamma, and Eva!

She returned home alone, but I was told nothing for several days. The tragic news was actually relayed to me in a singular manner. One evening, when I was almost falling asleep, Josephine came to my room.

"My father wants to see you."

How strange, I mused as I climbed out of bed. *Why would he wake me just as I was falling asleep?*

"You should know that Josephine went to fetch your sister, and to our sorrow she witnessed the arrest of your parents and sister," Josephine's father told me gravely. Then he walked off, leaving me to face my terrible grief in solitude.

The razor-sharp ache ripping through me as I digested the news could almost cut me in half. *What? My parents taken away?* The heavens crashed down on me at that moment. I felt as if I'd been severed from my source of life! My place in this world was no more.

Go and try to understand why this couldn't have waited for the next morning. Perhaps he thought if I was sleepy, my young mind would not completely assimilate the news at once and I would be slower to react.

From that moment, I became trapped in a chokehold of rage. Abandoned to my sorrow, with no one to vent to, no one I could share the enormity of my pain with, and all the while having to maintain the pretension of being a carefree, gentile child was beyond my seven-year-old level of endurance. I ran uncontrollably about in the surrounding fields, faster and faster, circling the fields dizzily. Where to flee to escape the anguish consuming my mind?

My host was concerned about me. Since the little village was close to the Dutch border, there was serious smuggling going on from Holland into Belgium — mainly butter, cheese, and eggs, vital food staples in light of the war shortages. It was feared that my erratic behavior would attract the attention of the Nazis, who often came in pursuit of the smugglers. Fearing that I would endanger myself as well as the host family, I was transferred back to the Jewish committee in Brussels, while my younger brothers remained in Essen for the duration of the war.

My First Encounter with My Hero

April 1943

I was eight and a half years old on *chol hamo'ed* Pesach 1943 when I first met Mr. Tiefenbrunner. I was living in a non-Jewish orphanage in Brussels in which the AJB had placed me. The orphanage was situated near a Jewish hospital. When the Allies had begun bombing Brussels, the premises of the neighboring Jewish hospital had been hit, and thus the patients were temporarily being housed in a wing of the orphanage. Occasionally I would visit the patients. One day, as I exited the gate of the temporary hospital quarters, I encountered a large man of Orthodox Jewish appearance.

He walked past me, my Aryan appearance momentarily confusing him — my hair was very blond, and I didn't have the look of a typical Jewish boy. He must have wondered what I was doing coming out of the Jewish hospital. He stopped and studied my face intently.

"What is your name, child?" he asked me gently.

"Did your parents have a shop for electrical supplies in Antwerp?" the man persisted after I had indicated my name.

"Yes!" I nodded exuberantly.

"I knew your father, Reb Sender Peterfreund! Both of our parents came from Sanz." He paused. "A wonderful Jewish boy can't stay here in this gentile orphanage!"

How to describe the wave of relief and elation that washed over me just then? *I am not just a number, a floundering orphan among so many other homeless boys,* I thought to myself. *Somebody knows I'm not just a boy from the street. Somebody knows who my family is, where I come from, to whom I belong!*

How to articulate the gratitude I was feeling to this man who had just validated my existence by recognizing my identity? He was a man I'd only just met, and yet in that instant his heart had become inextricably linked with my own.

True to his word, several weeks later Yona came to get me, along with another dozen Jewish boys and girls who were living in the non-

Jewish orphanage. Since his orphanage had no additional space, we were divided up among several of the other Jewish orphanages.

Returning Home after Liberation

January 1945

After the war, my uncle Saul Peterfreund (my father's youngest brother), his wife, Regina, and their daughter, Lilly, returned from Switzerland, where they had been hiding out during the war.

In June 1942, at the onset of the deportations, my uncle had asked my father to join them, but my father had declined. He had been stricken with food poisoning at the time and didn't want to endanger the escape with his ill health, and so my mother had decided to stay, too. Now, upon my uncle's return to Belgium, the first thing he did was to seek out survivors of the family. He went to Essen first and retrieved my two younger brothers — now ages 4 and 5, from their gentile foster family.

Although he and his wife attempted to take them in, it was a bit much for them amid the turmoil of reestablishing his own home, and so he sent them to the Mariaburg orphanage under the very reputable care of a family friend, Yona Tiefenbrunner.

Sometime later, I was located and taken in by my uncle and aunt.

Now that the war was over, it was time for me to think about going back to school. My aunt registered me in the sixth grade of Yesodei Hatorah. But first, I had to learn the *alef-beis* and to read all over again — my mind had been so tormented by the tragic events of the last few years that I had forgotten it all. My uncle hired a neighbor's son to tutor me and help me catch up.

Thus, I found myself back in the cheder that I had left four years ago — a lifetime ago — the day the school had been ordered to close. But alas, nobody recognized the spirited, feisty child I had been the day school closed in 1942. At eleven years old, I was an angry, embittered child, bent only on revenge on the gentiles for my parents' murders. After six months, when my uncle could no longer deal with my wild, obnoxious behavior, he sent me to live at the Mariaburg orphanage.

A New Lease on Life

April 1, 1946

I arrived on April 1, 1946. My two younger brothers had preceded me there already, so I joyfully reunited with them after three years.

Monsieur, as all the children referred to Yona Tiefenbrunner, greeted me warmly, as if reuniting with an old friend. But it was not immediate smooth sailing. My anger, my restlessness, my rebellion against authority prevented that. With gentility and sensitivity, Yona rose to the challenge of taming the tiger within me. He personified "*Rachmana liba bei* — Hashem, the Merciful One, desires you to have a heart." The warmth that emanated from him didn't — couldn't — leave me indifferent.

Gradually a wonderful understanding grew between us, and Monsieur succeeded in extricating me from the darkness and shadows of my painful emotions, which had virtually imprisoned me throughout that period. For the first time in years, I began to feel at peace with myself. I could feel hope. I could anticipate a future. Monsieur had given me a new lease on life.

Feeling at Home in My New World

April 1946

With my head and heart finally free, I was hungry for Torah learning and for the company of friends. I began attending the Gemara *shiur*. The new *chassidishe niggunim* I had learned from Reb Mendel Landau accompanied me everywhere — I was humming them all the time. Reb Mendel said they were legacies of the great Bobover Rebbes, of the dynasty that had begun in Sanz, my father's hometown.

One of the first Friday nights I spent in Mariaburg is still vivid in my memory. After we finished davening, we went out into the garden, into the warm spring evening. Joining hands, we formed a circle, moving round and round singing "*Shalom Aleichem.*" I can still sense the penetrating warmth of that harmonious circle, the circle that embraced the holiness of Shabbos, that embraced the eternity of *am Yisrael*, that embraced me as part of that eternity.

An embryonic feeling was taking root deep inside me: I was feeling at home in my new world.

My Bar Mitzvah Celebration and the Gift of a Jewish Homeland

November 30, 1947

I celebrated my bar mitzvah on *parashas Vayeishev*, the Shabbos before Chanukah. The night before, Friday, November 29, 1947, a historical meeting took place at Lake Success, New York. At that meeting, the United Nations General Assembly approved the plan for Jews to have a homeland. On Shabbos morning, after the *sheliach tzibbur* finished the *chazaras hashatz*, somebody shouted, "We ought to say Hallel!"

It was a great day, not only for me, but for all of *klal Yisrael*. It was a personal celebration, that I had been saved from the claws of the Nazi beasts, and on top of that we were now receiving such a wonderful present. You can imagine the euphoria of the people at my *simchah* — it was their *simchah*, too. After we finished davening, there was a nice *kiddush* and some *derashos,* and I received presents, mostly *sefarim*. This event will remain in my memory forever together with that famous November 29 declaration.

Growing in Gateshead

September 1953

Nineteen fifty-three, the year I spent in the Gateshead *yeshivah gedolah*, was a tremendous experience for me.

I had completed three years of business school. At the age of sixteen, upon the urging of my uncle Saul, I had begun attending the Antwerp School of Commerce to study bookkeeping and business administration. One Shabbos morning after davening, as my brothers and I were making our way to Uncle Saul for the Shabbos *seudah,* we encountered a relative of ours, Reb Yisroel Pesachovitz, a Gerrer chassid, a tzaddik of a Yid.

"What are you doing these days?" he inquired of me. When I told him that my uncle wanted me to attend business school, he dropped his tallis and ran ahead to my uncle's house.

"How can you send your brother's son among goyim?" he berated my uncle. "It's such a risk!"

My uncle calmed him down. "Don't worry," he reassured him. "He will still learn every day after school, and when he graduates, we will send him to Gateshead."

For three years I attended classes. During exam time, Monsieur would sit with me through the evenings into the wee morning hours like a true father — sometimes until one a.m. — assisting me with the difficult subject matter.

And then I was off to Gateshead. I spent a wonderful year basking in the pure and holy atmosphere under the *rosh yeshivah,* Rav Leib Gurwicz, and the *mashgiach*, Rav Moshe Shwab. They engendered in me such a *cheishek*, a passion for Torah learning.

All too soon my year of learning came to an end. I would have dearly loved to stay on, but my responsibility for my younger brothers weighed on me. I went back to Antwerp to look for work and to pursue my destiny of marriage and family.

Let the Story of This Great Giant Be Told

June 2000

Many years have passed since those days. I married in Israel and returned to Antwerp with my wife, where we established a family. Throughout, I maintained my connection with Monsieur. How shocked we were at the news of his untimely passing!

Recently one of the former boys of the Tiefenbrunner Home, now living in Israel, visited me. We spoke about writing a book about Monsieur. I had always harbored the deepest feelings of gratitude for the personal kindnesses Monsieur had done to me, for lifting me up from the depths.

But it was only now, years later, far removed from our daily connection with him, that we had become keenly aware of the phenomenon of his personality and the magnitude of his achievements, the impacts of which are still felt forty years later.

I remember a boy in the Mariaburg home by the name of Emanuel Tratner. He was extremely talented in drawing and had a copybook with him at all times in which he drew the most beautiful ships. Once, Monsieur initiated a conversation with us about what we intended to be in our adult lives.

"I want to be a policeman," Emanuel had answered. Monsieur made no comment, but the older ones among us knew Monsieur believed in more for his boys.

Years later, I was told that a certain Rav Emanuel Tratner was a *ram* in a prestigious yeshivah in Yerushalayim.

I told my son the other day that when I contemplate the scope of the activities and accomplishments of Mr. Tiefenbrunner during his short lifetime — the forty-eight years allotted to him — it appears that we are looking at the career of a man aged sixty or seventy. Monsieur had accomplished in those forty-eight years what most don't in double the number of years.

I want to thank my dear son, Yossel, for assisting me so trustfully day by day, enabling me to contribute somewhat to the homage of our dear "Monsieur," J. Tiefenbrunner, zt"l.

Bibliography

BOOKS:

Feldman, Alfred. *One Step Ahead: A Jewish Fugitive in Hitler's Europe.* Carbondale, Ill.: Southern Illinois University Press, 2001.

Michman, Dan, ed. *Belgium and the Holocaust: Jews, Belgians, Germans.* Jerusalem: Yad Vashem Publishing, 1998 .

Robinson Wayne, *Move Out, Verify: The Combat Story of the 743rd Battalion*. Frankfurt am Main: Heinrich, 1945.

Rosenblum, Yonasan. *They Called Him Mike: Reb Elimelech Tress.* New York: ArtScroll/Mesorah Publications, 2000.

Tiefenbrunner, Monju. *A Long Journey Home.* Jerusalem: 1999. Self-published.

ONLINE WEB LINKS:

Decoster, Charlotte, BA. "Jewish Children Hidden During the Holocaust: A Comparative Study of Their Hiding Places at Christian Establishments, Private Families, and Jewish Orphanages." Thesis prepared for master's degree, December 2006. http//www.digital.library.unt.edu/permalink/meta-dc-5468:1.

Oreck, Arden. "The Virtual Jewish History Tour Belgium." Jewish Virtual Library. http://www.jewish virtual library.org/jsource/vjw/Belgium.html.

The Jewish Museum of Deportation and Resistance. http://www.cicb.be/en/home_en.htm.

The World War II Living History Project. A high school educational project designed to collect and disseminate the personal histories of the World War II generation. http://www.hfcsd.org/ww2/WW2LHP%20homepage/Surveys/Civilian%20Survey%20v2.doc.

Wikipedia: The Free Encyclopedia. http://en.wikipedia.org/wiki.

INTERVIEWS AND LETTERS:

Personal interviews with Monsieur's immediate family members — three daughters and son in law, Joseph Schreiber, and elder brother Maurice (Monju) Tiefenbrunner.

Phone interviews with Miriam Zupnick's daughters.

Several personal interviews and phone and e-mail interviews with the former children of the home.

Letters and notes of tribute written by former children of the home upon the fortieth *yahrtzeit* of Monsieur.